# MY FAMOUS EVENING

# MY FAMOUS EVENING

*Nova Scotia Sojourns,*
*Diaries & Preoccupations*

# HOWARD NORMAN

NATIONAL GEOGRAPHIC DIRECTIONS

NATIONAL GEOGRAPHIC
*Washington, D.C.*

Published by the National Geographic Society
1145 17th Street, N.W., Washington, DC 20036-4688

Text copyright © 2004 Howard Norman
Map copyright © 2004 National Geographic Society

Photographs by Emma Norman

Library of Congress Cataloging-in-Publication Data

Norman, Howard A.
    My famous evening : Nova Scotia sojourns, diaries & preoccupations / Howard Norman.
        p. cm. -- (National Geographic directions)
    ISBN: 0-7922-6630-7
        1. Nova Scotia--Description and travel. 2. Nova Scotia--Social life and customs. 3. Nova Scotia--Biography. 4. Norman, Howard A.--Travel--Nova Scotia. 5. Authors, Canadian--Biography. I. Title. II. Series.

F1037.N57 2004
971.6--dc22

                                                        2003068603

One of the world's largest nonprofit scientific and educational organizations, the National Geographic Society was founded in 1888 "for the increase and diffusion of geographic knowledge." Fulfilling this mission, the Society educates and inspires millions every day through its magazines, books, television programs, videos, maps and atlases, research grants, the National Geographic Bee, teacher workshops, and innovative classroom materials. The Society is supported through membership dues, charitable gifts, and income from the sale of its educational products. This support is vital to National Geographic's mission to increase global understanding and promote conservation of our planet through exploration, research, and education.

For more information, please call 1-800-NGS LINE (647-5463), write to the Society at the above address, or visit the Society's Web site at www.nationalgeographic.com.

*Interior design by Melissa Farris*

*Printed in the U.S.A.*

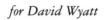

*for David Wyatt*

# CONTENTS

# MY FAMOUS EVENING

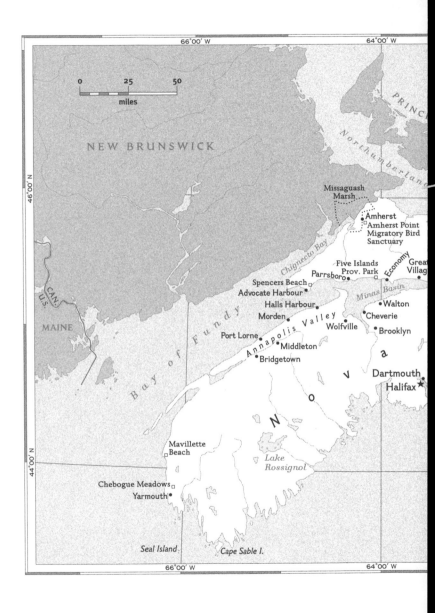

66°00′ W                                    64°00′ W

0        25        50
miles

NEW BRUNSWICK

PRINC

Northumberlan

46°00′ N

Missaguash
Marsh

Amherst
Amherst Point
Migratory Bird
Sanctuary

*Chignecto Bay*

Five Islands          Great
Prov. Park          Villag
Parrsboro                    Economy
Spencers Beach
Advocate Harbour              *Minas Basin*
Halls Harbour                      Walton
Morden                              Cheverie
                    Wolfville
Port Lorne          *Annapolis Valley*          Brooklyn
              Middleton
            Bridgetown                              a

MAINE

*Bay of Fundy*

CAN.
U.S.

N                v                Dartmouth
                                    Halifax

O

Mavillette
Beach                    *Lake
                        Rossignol*

44°00′ N

Chebogue Meadows
Yarmouth

Seal Island          Cape Sable I.

66°00′ W                                    64°00′ W

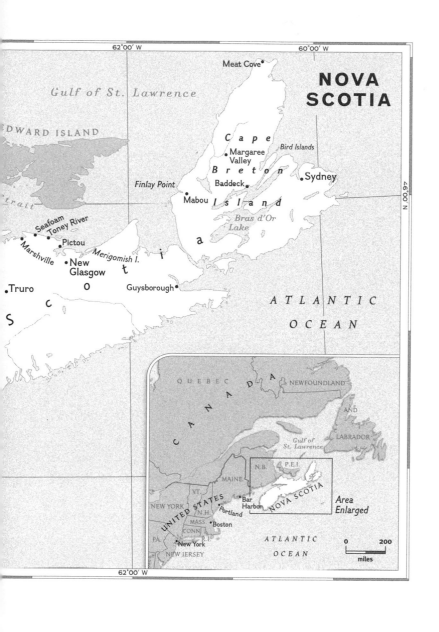

62°00′ W        60°00′ W

Meat Cove

Gulf of St. Lawrence

# NOVA
# SCOTIA

DWARD ISLAND

*C a p e*

Margaree
Valley    Bird Islands

*B r e t o n*

Finlay Point    Baddeck    Sydney

trait

Mabou   *I s l a n d*

Bras d'Or
Lake

Seafoam
Toney River

Pictou    *a*

Marshville   Merigomish I.

New
Glasgow   *t*

Truro    *O*    Guysborough

*c*

*S*

*A T L A N T I C*

*O C E A N*

QUEBEC    C   A   N   A   D   A    NEWFOUNDLAND

AND

LABRADOR

Gulf of
St. Lawrence

N.B.   P.E.I.

MAINE

VT.

NEW YORK

UNITED STATES   NOVA SCOTIA

N.H.    Bar
Harbor

Portland

MASS.

CONN.   Boston

R.I.

PA.

New York

NEW JERSEY

*Area
Enlarged*

*ATLANTIC*

*OCEAN*

0       200

miles

62°00′ W

*the bay coming in,*
*the bay not at home*

—ELIZABETH BISHOP
"The Moose"

*Are you for staying awake all night*
*to talk about this place? I'm up for*
*it, are you?*

—ANNIE DEWIS
Advocate Harbour, Nova Scotia, 1978

# INTRODUCTION

*Sudden Noir,
Deeper Calm*

IN 1979, I WAS HIRED TO WRITE A DOCUMENTARY FILM script, *Trotsky in Halifax.* The film never got made, but the research was a job well done, and allowed me to be apprised of yet another instance of history suddenly imposed on quotidian life. "Escorted by the authorities, yesterday the mysterious figure of Leon Trotsky suddenly arrived to our unsuspecting city," one journalist wrote, with a slightly anxious air of melodrama. "Tongues were set wagging, our citizenry rapt with alarming curiosity."

Why did Leon Trotsky pass through Halifax on his way to the October Revolution? In 1915, the Vitagraph Studio in New York hired émigré Emile Vester to direct *My Official Wife,* a WWI spy drama. I have seen this fierce, clumsy, noirish film. One crucial sequence depicts a band of embittered revolutionaries meeting in a dank basement. Vester had decided that in order to provide authentic Russian atmosphere, he needed "nihilistic" types as extras in this scene. To recruit, Vester simply walked into a Second Avenue café and offered its habitués five dollars a day for their work in a feature film. This is the exact point where the "fact" of a real personage and the "fiction" of a film scenario were inextricably bound, for among the volunteers who jumped at the chance for a screen appearance was Lev Bronstein—that is, Leon Trotsky. Trotsky had spent nearly a year in forced exile in New York editing the Bolshevik newspaper *Novy Mir (New World),* and the job with Vitagraph offered a welcome supplement to his meager salary. He appeared in the studio roster as "Mr. Brown." At one point in the film, if I recall correctly, Mr. Brown pounds the wall with his fist.

To my knowledge, *My Official Wife* was never shown in Halifax, at least not in any commercial theater. But on March 28, 1917, the Norwegian America Line ship *Kristianiafjord* steamed into Halifax Harbour from New York with a general cargo assigned to T. A. S. DeWolfe and Son. Tsar Nicholas II had only just abdicated, and the port authorities had received order to arrest eight passengers aboard the *Kristianiafjord*—one of them was Leon Trotsky.

Trotsky was taken before the military authorities, and a man named Dave Horwetz was assigned the duty of being Trotsky's official Russian interpreter. A document from the Naval Control Office, April 3, 1917, found in the Public Archives, is titled, "Russian Socialists on board the s.s. Kristianafjorde." The lengthy document itself says of Trotzki, Bronstein, age thirty-seven: "... traveling on card of Identity vised by the Russian Counsul at New York. He was President of the Workman's Delegations in Russia in 1905, was imprisoned for a time, but got away to Austria and was a journalist in Vienna till the commencement of the War: he then went to Switzerland and on to Paris, remaining there about 20 months, doing journalistic work. From Paris he went to New York, via Spain, and has continued the same vocation. He states that owing to the new regime in Russia he is returning to assist the Government. He makes no secret of his Socialist ideas, which appear to be very advanced, and he seems to have been in touch with Socialists of every nationality. He has a large amount of Socialistic literature in his possession. He claims acquaintance with the present Russian Minister for Foreign Affairs: he is accompanied by his Wife and two sons of 12 and 9."

From the Citadel in Halifax, Trotsky was removed to an internment camp in Amherst. His internment dragged on for nearly a month, during which, according to the *Halifax Herald,* he "raged, protested and hurled insults at the camp administration." There were at Amherst eight hundred German prisoners, many of them sailors of sunken submarines. Trotsky addressed them, explaining the ideas of Zimmerwald and telling them of the fight against the Kaiser and the war that Karl Liebknecht had been waging in Germany. The camp resounded with his speeches, and life in it changed into a "perpetual meeting." Finally, after much intrigue, bungling, and subterfuge, Trotsky left Amherst on April 29, followed to the gates of the camp by cheering German sailors and by the sounds of the "International" played by their orchestra.

During her husband's internment in Amherst, Mrs. Trotsky and her boys were ordered to remain in Halifax and given into the custody of Mr. Horwetz, who "took them to his humble home on Market Street." Accounts of Mrs. Trotsky and her sons in Halifax are quite wonderful, though some are nastily biased and require to be looked at askance. Reading of her daily walks around the city, one is toured through Halifax with vivid immediacy; her presence is noted as "historical," and one reporter even allows, "Seeing Halifax through this foreigner's eyes is seeing it somewhat anew, albeit at times unpleasantly." Mrs. Trotsky and sons watched workers passing into the boot and shoe factory of Robert Taylor and Company, which extended up Duke Street to Brunswick Street;

this five-story brick structure "was considered to be a first-class factory with light, airy rooms and modern machinery, and later was used by J. and M. Murphy for the manufacture of clothing." On Saturdays they watched horses and oxen toiling up the hill from the Dartmouth ferry, pulling market carts loaded with produce to be sold at the City Market, as the new market building had opened in July 1916 to replace the old Green Market held on the streets by the post office.

Mrs. Trotsky could speak Russian, German, and French, but as Horwetz reported, her English vocabulary consisted of three words: "Speak you French?" While at the Horwetz house, she was bitter in her denunciation of her "house arrest," insisting that she and her husband had committed no crime, were victims of the Tsar's agents through the British and American governments, and once back in Russia intended to "denounce Canada" as well. Finally, Mrs. Trotsky and sons were allowed to take rooms in the Prince George Hotel on the southeast corner of Sackville and Hollis Streets.

There is one especially telling anecdote, having to do with Mrs. Trotsky's wish to buy a writing pad. Mrs. Horwetz, who accompanied Mrs. Trotsky almost everywhere, and Mrs. Trotsky went directly to Connolly's Book and Stationery Store on Barrington Street, where the clerk showed Mrs. Trotsky a pad that had the entwined flags of the Allies emblazoned on the cover.

"I want none of them," she was said to have exclaimed in Russian. "I have no use for any flags, but the flag of real freedom!" Fortunately, as one article put it, "the clerk did not understand Russian."

Trotsky left Halifax on May 3 aboard the Scandinavian-American liner *Helig Olav,* en route to Copenhagen, allowed to sail only after a message from Kerensky, the war minister, had been received by British authorities urging that he be released to return to Russia.

As I've mentioned, the documentary was never filmed. Yet during the research I had conversations with collectors of Trotsky memorabilia, historians of international law, and quite a few people who remembered Trotsky's presence in Halifax, including one woman who had personally met Mrs. Trotsky. Day after day, night after night, I read about rumored plots to assassinate Trotsky, copied into a notebook fiery newspaper rhetoric, beneath which I knew had run a real current of political anxiety. A Mrs. Eddy, age eighty-three, said, "Goodness, all those foreign languages heard in the street!" (Perhaps all emanating from the Trotsky entourage!) In one newspaper article or other, I caught the phrase "the ship waiting to carry this Russian-Jewish revolutionary into the rapidly turning pages of History." Finally, one late night as I looked across the harbor to the bleak edifice of the Nova Scotia Hospital and surrounding lights of Dartmouth, weeks of obsessing about

Trotsky in Halifax instilled in me what Graham Greene called "a sudden noir of the heart." It was a penetrating, ghostly sensation that the wind, the fog, the water, the old buildings of the Historic District, still carried voices from 1917, and that the city of Halifax would never relinquish its secrets easily. Naturally, the history of Halifax, like that of any city, contains opposing forces. As George Elliott Clark put it, "Halifax has some wild mysteries, some bad things have happened here, and not everything's been written down yet. Beautiful city, though. Good people. Good town."

Researching Trotsky in Halifax also allowed me a framework within which to think about "atmosphere," useful to later writing, especially of novels. To this day when I step from the Haliburton House Inn and walk down Morris Street to the harbor, I'm given to the possibility of experiencing a "sudden noir of the heart." I wish the ghosts of 1917 would start talking so I could eavesdrop. Such thinking is by now natural to my character, habitual, sustaining. I am not a Haligonian; I am, however, as often as possible a visitor to Halifax, my favorite city. And part of why Halifax is my favorite city is its hospitality and even its indecipherable indifference to my particular imagination, ponderings, literary investigations.

I think of the summer of 1979, too, as a time in which a city-rural axis fell into place, and, what's more, while researching *Trotsky in Halifax,* I actually kept to a schedule: Tuesday, Wednesday, Thursday I worked in Halifax, writing at night in my room at the Lord Nelson Hotel. On Friday, Saturday, Sunday, and Monday, I lived in a big, ramshackle house in Advocate Harbour, on the Bay of Fundy, compliments of the playwright Sam Shepard. Sam and I had met in San Francisco, did a reading together at Intersection; subsequently he offered me use of his house in Advocate Harbour. A letter he sent me offered detailed directions, a loving description of a neighbor, Scott Dewis, a warning, and advice. "The well is located in the back porch & I'd check it for dead mice before you start drinking the water," he wrote. "The lobster season should be on by the time you arrive. And you can always get fresh lobster & boil them in a bucket. Really delicious. Ask Scott about where to pick some 'Fiddle Neck Greens' or 'Goose Tongue Greens'—they're all a real delicacy."

Back and forth, weekly, for three months, then, I drove the jeep out of Advocate Harbour along the Glooskap Trail to Truro, growing familiar with the villages, the landscape, the birds. I would then have lunch in Truro and continue south on 102 to Halifax. In 1984 my wife, poet Jane Shore, and I took our honeymoon in Nova Scotia. We drove from Halifax to the Margaree Valley, stayed at the Normaway Inn (still owned and operated by Dave Macdonald, whom I consider a local historian). We had a day before our reservation to catch the seven-hour *Bluenose* ferry out of Yarmouth, across to Bar Harbor, Maine.

We decided to drive along Route 2, along the Bay of Fundy, and stop at Great Village, where the poet Elizabeth Bishop had spent part of her childhood in the home of her maternal grandparents. Eventually Ms. Bishop would set a number of remarkable poems and memory-pieces there. Jane had been a colleague of Elizabeth Bishop's at Harvard and very much wanted to see this ancestral home. We more or less simply dropped in, and received a warm welcome from Mrs. Hazel Bowers, a distant relative of Bishop's who was then living in the house. Hazel had taught school in Nova Scotia for thirty-two years; for nine years before her retirement she was principal of the Great Village School, which Elizabeth Bishop attended in 1916-17 (during which time a young man from Great Village had the duty of guarding Trotsky en route to Halifax). Hazel gave us a tour, served tea, and offered to put us up for the night, which we politely declined; later Jane remarked, more than halfway serious, "What if I saw her ghost?"

The small house was located directly across from the old Esso gas station. A few days before our visit, the station had suffered a fire; ironic, to say the least, since Bishop's poem "Filling Station" contains the line, *Be careful with that match!*

Standing on the side porch, I thought of how often I had driven past this very house, totally ignorant of its history and meaning. I didn't mention it, mainly out of embarrassment. Well, things come round and round: eighteen years later almost to the day, I traveled with Jane, our fourteen-year-old daughter, Emma, her friend Millan, and Bishop's childhood biographer, Sandra Barry, from Halifax to Great Village. (See "Driving Miss Barry," p. 141.) Unloading eleven pieces of luggage at the Blakie House in Great Village, looking at Emma taking out her camera in order to chronicle her parents' return and her introduction to this splendid village, the "timeless" backdrop of field and woods leading out to the Bay of Fundy, I thought to myself (with tiresome irony), "Well, some things naturally change and some don't."

As for human beings in general, unless one is of Mi'kmaq Indian blood, all Nova Scotians, whether of Scottish, German, African, Irish, or French ancestry, are "come-from-away." Some families of European descent go back many generations, of course. In this light, since I first visited Nova Scotia in 1969, I must consider myself still in the fledgling "tourist" category, and perhaps always should. Some of my own ancestors, Russian and Polish Jews, those desperately inventive and fortunate enough to flee pogroms and fascism, landed for short periods in Halifax before moving on to points west in Canada and into the United States. But I can hardly claim provenance, and wish to avoid that fraudulent suggestion at all costs. I have always visited Nova Scotia, lived in Nova Scotia, because it is the place, with the exception of Vermont, I simply am most comfortable. Much has to do with the landscape and birds. And, over the last fifteen years, the writing of novels, which means that the actual experience of being *in* Nova Scotia is well-met with my imagining Nova Scotia in absentia. In turn, mornings when I am indeed in Nova Scotia, I often wake to immediately look out on the very landscape I'd been dreaming about; that is, the distance between unconscious and conscious is scarcely noticeable. At such moments one feels perhaps most fully realized.

*My Famous Evening* is a book of selective memories. In terms of its literary nature, I adhere to Emily Dickinson's advice, to "tell it slant." Trying to find the most useful and gratifying angle of approach to the subject of "place," as with any writing, involves the strenuous matters of form, style, what to include, what to leave out, what should metaphorically resonate and what should be described in almost purely expository prose. My belief is that, as Dylan Thomas said, "a book is like a life, most poignantly viewed by holding it up to the light, slowly turning it, catching its angles, but feeling the substance of the whole." *My Famous Evening* is at least structured so that its chapters may be seen as intersecting facets of reminiscence: There are certain refrains, themes, preoccupations, and I placed birds in as many of the book's nooks and crannies as possible. The book is divided into four chapters. Chapter One, "My Famous Evening," has to do with the life and letters of Marlais Quire, a young woman who in 1923 left her home in Nova Scotia and traveled down to New York, in the decidedly ill-fated attempt to see the famous writer Joseph Conrad read from his works. Chapter Two, "Life, Death, and the Sea: Forerunners and Divinations," features the collecting of various categories of folklore and plaits in failed romance to boot. Chapter Three, "A Birder's Notebook," is an homage to the Bay of Fundy and the Mi'kmaq hero-giant, Glooskap, and provides a few Mi'kmaq folktales about Glooskap. In Chapter Four, "Driving Miss Barry," my ambition was—simply put—to profile a remarkable woman, researcher-historian-poet Sandra Barry, to characterize spending time with her in and around Great Village, a place she has written eloquently about, and allow Sandra, mainly via conversations, to provide a sort of "memoir." The brief epilogue, "Robert Frank Equals Late Autumn," comprises an October day's collage-diary, a day during which the writer is solely preoccupied with the landscape photographs of the great Robert Frank. I entitled it "Robert Frank Equals Late Autumn" because I find a correspondence between the severe melancholy of these photographs and the mood engendered by the landscape, bleak weather, and light in October, November, and into early December in Cape Breton, more specifically along the Northumberland Strait as it opens northward into the Gulf of St. Lawrence.

Since no book can "define" Nova Scotia (certainly no book I could write), I merely asked of myself in which ways can years of diaries, journals, tape recordings, jottings-down of this and that sort be best organized and presented, to at least provide some of the emotional dimensions of my experiences? I came to the conclusion that I'd try to contextualize a sense of Time by weaving as many people's stories as possible into my own. That is why, for instance, there are so many quotation marks in the chapter "Life, Death, and the Sea." I simply wanted a reader to *hear* some of the voices I heard, to hear people talk about superstition, fate, and belief. Likewise, in the chapter "Driving Miss Barry," I quote at length from conversations along-the-road with Sandra, because she says things at heartfelt best and most succinctly.

October 2002, on a sojourn to Cape Breton, I stopped at Telegraph House on Chebucto Street in Baddeck, an establishment built in 1861. It was where Alexander Graham Bell stayed when he first came to Baddeck. I visited, like any good tourist, the Alexander Graham Bell National Historic Site. As the brochure informs us, "Each summer for much of his life, noted inventor Alexander Graham Bell fled the heat of Washington, D.C., for a hillside retreat high above Bras d'Or Lake. The mansion, which is still owned and occupied by the Bell family, is visible across the harbor from various spots around town." Bell invented the telephone at age twenty-nine. But the museum contains Bell's "less-lauded inventions" as well: ingenious kites, hydrofoils, airplanes. Out near the mansion, I pondered in no original way about the network of thought brought about by the invention of the telephone. In the midst of this brief meditation, a cell phone jangled my nerves, and I

scowled at a fellow tourist, who in turn seemed per-
plexed, shrugging, "What's with you?" (Or more to the
point, "Which century do you think you're living in?")
It's not the invention, of course, it's which altruistic or
mindless use it is put to.

One of my students writing about John Lennon gave me
a postcard miniaturizing a gun-control billboard signed
by Yoko Ono. It reads, "Over 676,000 people have been
killed by guns in the U.S.A. since John Lennon was shot
and killed on December 8, 1980." I mention this in particular because, during that October sojourn to Nova
Scotia, the now infamous "snipers" were at work in
Washington, D.C., where my wife teaches and my
daughter goes to school. Amid the physical beauty of
autumn Nova Scotia, I often felt my stomach twisting
up, until I heard on the radio that these soulless men
had been apprehended. But living in Washington,
D.C., means I live (albeit part of the year) in a place of
murder. Though my true home is Vermont, which
does not generally feel like a place of murder, that is,
a preponderance of murderous crime does not keep its
citizens just short of nervous shock—"murder does not
visit here but rarely," as Thoreau put it, about another
time and place in America. Meandering the October

roads in Nova Scotia, then, was to still dwell within the inescapable dualism of existence in the new century: To feel peaceful in one's heart (say if you live in an American city), one must go to "another place." Alas, I feel fortunate to spend extended periods in Vermont and Nova Scotia, which, in my life, offer corresponding dignities.

Since 1969, I have been a tourist in Nova Scotia in basically two ways. First, I have often signed on for actual tours, such as the "ghost tour" in Halifax, with its stops at various places said to have been, or still be, haunted by ghosts. That was a delightful experience. One summer at my own pace, I visited every lighthouse in the province. Of course, lighthouses and their individual architectures and histories were simply the organizing principle; the real "reason" for this travel was to see things along the way, to feel "unmoored within reason," as Emerson said, to meander a bit, to see what was around the bend, to wonder, as in a good novel, what was to happen next. I have paid good money to be lectured about gravestones and grave-markings in the cemeteries of Halifax, even studied up by reading *Titanic Victims in Halifax Graveyards,* by Blair Beed. To this end, I highly recommend *Life How*

*Short, Eternity How Long,* a book on gravestone carving and carvers in Nova Scotia, by Deborah Trask. In Wolfville near the Annapolis Valley, I paid the price of a ticket to hear an enterprising college student recite the entirety of *Evangeline,* the melodramatic epic of lovers torn asunder by the Acadian expulsions of 1755, written by Henry Wadsworth Longfellow. (As she sang for her tuition, as it were, I sat next to a tense fellow following every line in a weather-beaten copy of the poem; I had the distinct feeling that any skipped-over word or botched line might result in his demand for a refund.) I went to see where Adèle Hugo, daughter of Victor Hugo, lived in Halifax; I even trustingly purchased what turned out to be a forged letter from Adèle Hugo. (I did not press charges.) And then there have been a multitude of specifically oriented journeys to see birds, a few of which unexpectedly provided— past the more predictable solace of birding—some spiritual heightening, and in retrospect felt like pilgrimages. This past October, for the first time, I attended the wonderful Celtic Colours International Festival, nine days of "driving fiddles, skirling bagpipes, dancing feet and voices joined together in song," whose information officer, Dave Mahalik, kindly offered me a special pass to events. To hear musicians such as Brittany's Patrick and Jacky Molard was to certainly be transported.

Second, I have written about Nova Scotia—mainly its natural history—to make a living. This began in 1970, and over the years my employers have varied from travel sections of newspapers to radio, to museums, to film companies. Not only would I be remiss not to consider *My Famous Evening* as part of that trajectory, but I am specifically grateful to National Geographic Directions editor Elizabeth Newhouse for asking me to write it.

Also in October 2002, to my great surprise, I was asked to participate in an evening forum, "Sense of Place," sponsored by Mary Stinson's excellent CBC Radio program, *Writers & Company*. The singular warmth and forbearance of writers such as George Elliot Clarke (whose collection *Blue* strikes me as one of our most powerfully unique meditations on race, history, and literary imagination, and that hardly does it justice), and Alistair MacLeod, was heartening. Mary's questions were thoughtful, not at all run-of-the-mill, and the audience commensurately so. Perhaps this is wishful thinking in retrospect, but as the evening progressed I was not given to feel, as an American writer, the odd man out, not in the least. As the conversation meandered toward its end, the question was put to us, "How would you define 'home?'" Alistair MacLeod, who all along had been, as hoped, a seasoned, charming raconteur, let his voice register a matter-of-fact yet nonetheless wistful tone. "Oh, I can't think of any other end for me but to be buried in Cape Breton," he said. "That would be coming home. So in a sense it would be a definition of 'home,' you see." Taking his lead, similar sentiments were offered by the other panelists. (I wanted to be buried in Vermont.) Each writer had traveled widely, lived in a number of places, and bemoaned a certain restlessness and, at the same time, a longing to stay put. (I think here of Robert Frank's advice often scrawled on a photograph, HOLD STILL — KEEP MOVING.) Each panelist in turn delegated the most emotional authority to where one "ends up," as if by tidal pull of fate, rather than where one necessarily lives one's entire life. That was very moving indeed.

For and about the book you now hold in your hand, I shall neither apologize nor claim invaluable circumspection; I hope that there is some enjoyment to be found in it. If I haven't always got the name of a river correctly, I trust you'll know that I tried at least to get the sound and light of the river across—verisimilitude is mandatory, the imparting of facts, as memory allows, responsible, and I tried for both in equal measure, if that is possible. There, too, were certain things I very much wanted to write about, but could not quite discover how they would modestly comport themselves in these pages. Such as seeing a vagabond flock of tundra swans—where exactly had they come from, why had they wandered off-course?—at Advocate Beach. Such as the woman I met in Truro whose elderly, mute mother in her youth had participated in the robbing of a train—in India. Such as an amazing account of a married man who was a member of the Nova Scotia Fruit Growers' Association and participated with that group in the 1893 World's Fair in Chicago. While in Chicago, he fell in love with and secretly married an American woman, and began essentially—in terms of marriage, at least—a dual citizenship. However, when the Chicago wife discovered that there was a Nova Scotian wife, she felt compelled to reveal *her* other husband, a missionary doctor working in Cairo, Egypt. Such as the Séance Book Club I attended in a hotel on Prince Edward Island, wherein the participants, most of whom had traveled to the island from mainland Nova Scotia, "channeled" the voices of a book's characters, giving them the opportunity to criticize or praise how their lives were written. I just couldn't get these stories down correctly. Not to put too fine a point on it, but a writer must be vigilant against ostentatious, let alone indiscrete entries. Mostly I wanted to turn certain stories over to readers just as I'd been entrusted with them.

Nova Scotia is strange in my life: It provides a sudden noir of the heart, just as it does the deepest calm. Emotions seesaw. There are exhaustions and exhilarations in all of this, love and confusion, obsession and wonder. Nova Scotia has long been for me the one place I get the uncanny sense of missing, even as I am firmly standing on its ground, breathing its air, squinting against its hard sunlight off water. Just as I miss Nova Scotia this very moment as I write.

Halifax, 2003

CHAPTER ONE

*My Famous*
*Evening*

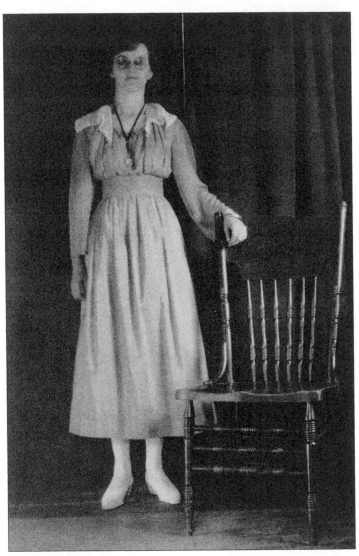

*Mrs. Marlais Quire in 1921*

THE FOLLOWING STORY ABOUT A WOMAN NAMED Marlais Quire is the one I am most grateful to have heard; hers are the letters I am most grateful to have read.

Decades before Alistair MacLeod composed his inimitable Cape Breton stories, George Elliot Clark his powerful lyric sequence, *Whylah Falls* in "the Afro-Nova Scotian *Africadian* vernacular," and Elizabeth Bishop "The Moose"—a haunting, great poem set along the Bay of Fundy, replete with narrator Miss Bishop eavesdropping in on the afterlife a few seats behind her on a bus—world literature arrived to Nova Scotia in 1921, in the form of two novels by Polish-born Joseph Conrad. These were *Nostromo,* published in 1904, and

*Twixt Land and Sea,* published in 1912. In 1922 a woman named Mary Abernathy brought both novels home from London to near Guysborough, an outport on the Atlantic side of the province. She had a younger sister, Marlais—her maiden name was Marlais Abernathy—a dedicated reader.

Marlais read the two novels within a week. "After that," Mary, age eighty-five, told me, on a sunny day in July 1974, at a rented bungalow on St. Andrews Channel, Cape Breton Island, "my sister was changed. I mean in the way someone lovesick is changed; you either get married or throw yourself into the sea." She laughed heartily. "Or you do what my brave, foolish sister did, don't you? You leave home and go to one of the biggest cities in the world, then you come back and bear up under whatever the consequences of your leaving."

Early in 1922, Mary wrote to her London friends, requesting another novel by Joseph Conrad, and when *The Nigger of the Narcissus,* published in 1897, arrived, Marlais devoured it as well. "She read them each any number of times," Mary said. "Late at night, as her marriage allowed."

By 1923 Alfonse Quire, Marlais's husband, was thirty-nine and Marlais was twenty-seven. Alfonse was known as a taciturn man. "Dour at his most buoyant," is how Mary put it, with stinging irony. "I didn't care much for him, but I kept that to myself." Marlais and

Alfonse had two children, Donald and Mary (named after her aunt), ages nine and six, respectively. "My sister and her husband had a storm-in-a-bottle marriage," Mary said.

One night early in March 1923, Marlais and Alfonse had a terrible row. According to the third letter Marlais Quire sent, the quarrel primarily was about her intention to travel alone to New York City, where she hoped to attend a reading by Joseph Conrad, a rare appearance of the enigmatic literary giant during his only visit to America. Mary had received a letter from her friends "who kept up on such things" in London, which included a notice of Joseph Conrad's invitation and acceptance, published in the *Times*. "Perhaps my sister was looking for a reason to take leave of Alfonse for a while," Mary said. "I think that was at least partly true. But I know she thought it would be a once-in-a-lifetime thing. Life at home was all child-rearing and sameness, of course. Which naturally provides much good in life. And Marlais was not selfish in that respect. She was a dutiful wife. But then she certainly took a journey out, didn't she? Look at the letters she wrote to me! How those books affected her!"

After some small talk, Mary set a tin candy box on the splintery kitchen table. She had been delivered to the bungalow by her nephew, Scott. Every now and then I glanced over and saw him leaning against the pickup truck, or sitting in the front seat, door swung open, smoking a cigarette.

"Well, here they are," she said. Her sister's letters were wrapped in twine. "These are the letters I told you about. The ones my sister sent me, when she went off to try and see Mr. Conrad in New York City. Go ahead, read them. They're written in pencil, as you see. I've ordered them as they were sent and arrived."

I read the first letter:

My dearest Mary,

As you know better than anyone, dear sister, I've scarcely had an eventful life, and yet I have been away from home 16 days now and wait here in the city of Halifax hoping to book passage to New York in America to see the great writer Joseph Conrad. This you already know, from our conversations, dear one, so I won't linger on that elemental.

Presently I have a room at The Baptist Spa and it is affordable. Yet I restrict myself to a mid day meal and tea whenever I wish. Passage was indeed booked right away, but then I lost my booking to, I believe, a relative of someone in the shipping company. Oh how the world works sometimes, fine for the topic of a sermon in church but not so fine for a woman whose passage was stolen out from under her very nose, now, is it? Yet I've been promised a new booking and will anyway go to the shipping office daily. I am resourceful. I know which ships are possible, because the newspaper posts schedules on the Shipping Page, which I get in the public reading room here. I could fairly live in the library here, which I have visited twice already, and what a comfort! By now I am of low reputation at home. How could it be otherwise? By now my husband and children are greatly shamed, in the knowledge that in addition to leaving hearth and home for selfish purposes, I had taken the sum of 28 from the church box of which I was the custodian. 28 which went directly to my costs of travel. And while I have little doubt as to my ability to pay this debt at first possible opportunity, even if penny by penny, I most likely will spend some time in prison, since forgiveness in our Christian response cannot but work at cross purposes with the law. This is my confession to you alone, dear Mary, that when I took the 28 I knew exactly why—because I would be more secure in my travels because of it. I am clear headed and see it still as a practical matter. And I fully expect the practicality of the law to respond in kind. As for now, I sit and have tea and speak to you as if you sit across the table, as we would almost daily in our sisterly fealty and love. Yet of course I sit alone, in the city of Halifax. I trust, Mary dear, that you keep the novels authored by Mr. Joseph Conrad and the others well out of harm's way, that is out of Alfonse's reach, of course, as I have asked. Dear one, you could not have possibly foreseen this. You have always been my source of hope and encouragement, and supplied me with literature. I am more grateful than ever. I can name every book you have given me. And yet I can say outright dear one it was the novels particularly of Mr. Joseph Conrad put me out in the world as I now am. Far away from hearth and home as I now am and no doubt won't return to as I knew them before. To some I'm sure Mr. Conrad writes adventure tales, whereas to me he writes waking dreams such as makes it possible to see, hear and even however wanly I manage this, philosophize differently. His writing helps me move forward in my thinking, which I'm afraid was evident to Alfonse—I wanted it to be!—and which therefore provided a dire prospect I'm sure for the poor husband! There is a place in my heart for our sisterly conversations which is not possible to be found by any mortals but one another. God may have listened in at moments of specific curiosity about which subjects sisters speak about, long after the husbands and children are in bed asleep, otherwise all are secrets forever kept, be sure of it. I am here in Halifax and will book passage to New York, and that, dear one, is really all

I know just now, except that whatever hours of peaceful sleep I might manage will be allowed by the knowledge that you will kiss my children for me and say to them that someday they will understand. That no matter what has persuaded me away from them is temporary. That they must learn to love books and despise convenient ignorance of books, that they must adore the librarian Mrs. Spivey well past her stormy temperment, for all she provides. I have had my mid day meal and tea, and shall post this. In plainest possible meaning, I am your loyal and loving sister.

Marlais Abernathy

"Take note," Mary said, "that my sister signed her first letter Marlais *Abernathy,* and signed every one of them the same. In her mind she'd divorced Alfonse at the earliest possible moment, eh?—or went back to a time before the marriage."

After I set down the first letter, Mary said, "My sister really had no reason to write letters before. Everyone she knew lived nearby. As far as I know, these were the only letters she ever wrote in her entire life!"

Mary closed her eyes. "I can sleep sitting up like this," she said. "Carry on with your reading, then."

My dearest sister,

I might well suppose that by now the authorities have delivered the dread news that my husband Alfonse is killed. He was not killed directly by my hand but indirectly by my inability to calm him in front of The Baptist Spa, where he waved a revolver and shouted, "You are my wife!—" followed by cursing so violent that my fear was tempered only by the familiarity of his bellowing voice, though the circumstances were not now familiar at all. He had somehow located my whereabouts—on what funds did my husband travel down, I wonder, as he was not a man to borrow money—and waited for me on the steps of The Baptist Spa, immediately to bellow marriage complaints. In Halifax at that time of evening at this time of year apparently fog rolls up from the harbour some nights so thickly all walking the street may as well carry a blindman's cane, and I'm told that that is little exaggerated. But the fog was only beginning up from the harbour when I was confronted by my husband. Dear dearest sister, I had just left The Baptist Spa to walk down to see one of the new Birney cars, which I very much wished to see. Birney cars run on tracks. I intended to invest in a ride on one no matter my finances. And there stood Alfonse. Or I should better say there he stood but not stood still as he was shuffling like erasing a chalk hopscotch game with his boots on the sidewalk as in the one we saw in the magazine you had displayed at your house, Mary, remember? At first he could not meet my eye and then he met it with the Devil's eyes not his own which I imagine was due to drink. He smelled of drink and he actually said as much, he said, "I've been at the bottle!" You yourself have seen him at the bottle you know what that means. "Put the revolver away, Alfonse," I said. I said "I won't invite you in but we can sit on the steps or walk or anything you wish!" "You won't invite your own husband in? Then who am I to you?" I knew I had chosen the wrong words and the curses started up then and there he was convicting me of all manner of transgression and selfishness as a wife and I hadn't even gotten to street level yet. Oh my Lord my very soul felt precarious and I did not know my husband at all, Mary, not at all. I did not know him as if the fog had moved across and erased him from my life and perhaps I wished somehow for that to happen, Lord help me, I won't be forgiven for that thought will I? Obviously our shouting drew the attention of two policemen not more than a hop skip and jump away and the good policemen did not shirk their duty and approached us. Alfonse might better have thrown his revolver to the ground and pointed it out there and said "Good fellows, this is my wife and this is an unfortunate private matter mistakenly out in public," but instead he waved it and shot it into the air. There immediately ensued in a blur and a curse a terrible scuffle and Alfonse perhaps innocent at all costs in the ways of the city might better not have resisted. In these terrible moments my face was bruised and I fled, a cowardly act of which I am not a little ashamed and running heard a pistol shot ring out. I feel that my unhappiness in marriage and impetuousness in travel had contributed to my husband's death at that very instant and my children became half orphaned. And yet I am still on to New York and having so continued in this endeavor, my dear one, what chance does my soul have for Heaven? I have the dress coat shoes and the rest that I am wearing. They are my only ownership. My suitcase is on the bed in my room at The Baptist Spa and I don't dare retrieve it. All other worldly belongings consist of the clearest sight of you my dear sister and my children in my mind. I have told you something here that I wish were a dream but is whatever the opposite of a dream may be. What is the one thing good in my nature which is my love of books has put me it seems in the worst of circumstances. I am selfish in all regards except for my love of you and my children which sustains me. Please kiss them for me as I expect you would anyway without my asking dear dear dearest. I am selfish in all regards except for my love of you and them. In all regards to be sure, but I felt that after twelve years of contentious marriage my stalwart reading habits mocked at table, losing two children before birth it was all this and more and the possibility of experiencing a moment of the highest spiritual order outside of church—hearing Mr. Conrad, that had allowed me to cast aside all best notions of redemption and now look at the consequences, my children half orphaned, father gone, mother unmoored, aunt saying nightly prayers with them. Now look at me, your sister, I am on the lam. All angels previously disappointed in me since girlhood are now ten-fold now more and fully vindicated in their disappointment. In persistent memory and love,

Marlais Abernathy

As it turned out, Alfonse merely had a bullet lodged in his thumb. After the bullet was removed in hospital, he spent two days in jail, during which time he had contact with no one but his jailers. Finally, he was severely reprimanded in front of both policemen, fined a modest amount for the equivalent, I suppose, of disturbing the peace, then sent packing to nearby Whale Cove in Cape Breton Island. There he retained—whether by some legal procedure or otherwise, I do not know—custody of his children. In the ensuing years, Alfonse, according to Mary, "continued employment as a jack-of-all-trades, a carpenter generally hired out. Not entirely a lazy man, Alfonse, but not all that hardworking, either.

"But now he had a wife with a shameful past—or his past had a shameful wife. I think he saw it both ways."

Dearest Mary,

Please kiss my children for me. I have finally booked passage, the ship is called SST Hoag carrying freight and mail and I believe there are several motor cars aboard and four small rooms for passengers aside from crew. "Weep into the rainy sea-wind/for the rainy sea-wind is discrete for private weeping—" remember that verse mother would read when we became upset over something or other? It was indeed raining much of the morning, this. The ship docked for repairs or whatnot in Portland Maine and myself and others debarked for ten hours time, we were told we could go on into town and stay the night as we were guaranteed the repairs would take that long at least. I know that a Mr. and Mrs. Rhineman purchased a room for the night just up from the modest wharf. I found a place to have tea and soup and then was happy for it being balmy because I would be up awake in it all night. I found a church not of our denomination but its door was open and I went in, the pews were comfortable and I slept fitfully but slept, a blessing to be sure, having the church to myself till morning. Yet much to my embarrassed surprise it was then a Sunday morning and I was awakened by a parishioner and so sat through the service, which was foreignly pleasant. No matter how familiar or not the type of sermon, I always get spent in church. I recall certain Sundays I was exhausted by merely the normal goings-on nearly to the point of fainting—just the sermon itself, just people standing up or sitting down, the sameness. I have generally always loved the sermons but have always since childhood I think reserved a contentious attitude toward them and what they attempt to persuade us of our natures. As for sin, what, for instance, did my children ever do to deserve such a mother, but be born and begin a life? What, Mary dear, did you ever do but be born and have a life? Born sinner, born sinner—yes, perhaps that is me, perhaps it is, but I'm more convinced of that particular trait on days of ill temper than happiness. On bright sunny days I have tended to think that we all were born innocent and the first blanket laid over us in our cribs were woven of possibility rather than Fate. Oh I don't know what

I think just now, anyway, except my back hurts terribly from sitting up in the hard pew. Anyway, townsfolk surrounded me in church this morning, all seemed gentle and sincere in their prayers and hymns and as the hymns resounded around me I wondered if Alfonse Quire had already been buried and wept over yet. I suppose he had already been borne up to those disappointed angels already, if that's where he was borne up to in fact. I used to laugh to myself about his name—Quire—and would often have a play on words in my mind, saying, "Oh he'll never sing in one, not at least a Heavenly choir!" Our last quarrel which was our last truly married night in the kitchen of our house haunts me up to and through this very moment, dear sister, and shall I imagine well past it. It often more or less uncoils in my mind, how I was pleading what harm is done that I should hear a great man of literature read from his works if it were possible to do so? I would simply travel out and back on my own fortitude my wits about me, and out and back and be done with it, and if I were only to have this wish fulfilled why would not a husband help fulfill it, wishing for the same on my behalf. Looking back I no doubt simplify things—no doubt!

Alfonse, as you know, could not read but further he did not even enjoy my summaries of books I had read, during he would sit there hunched in a chair as though receiving blows. To each his own, I suppose, but in marriage certain separate passions may come about and mine was scarcely tolerated and now look at me in a few short weeks your sister has become a woman sleeps in churches, washes in public washrooms and who presently suffers a chill and posts letters from far away. Naturally and in good taste I write only to you, Mary, and I trust the address is not too much labor a walk and that word from the widow Mrs. Gale that a letter has arrived is not part of gossip but of private arrangement as she promised. I trust that is so. I went to the public library here and found that Mr. Conrad has written even more volumes than I previously knew! but they will have to wait. But I shall get to them. In the library I read poetry and one poem in particular whose subject was a lost soul, which read in part—"Sea-faring the pure and righteous one could survive on a crust of bread and the air of hope and certainty of God/but I of The Other Path/ Of hardened heart, have stolen a loaf of bread from the bakery" and reading this, I was startled. This is me. I am of The Other Path. Having stolen from my church box. I think, truth be told, I am seeing things through a fever now, because a short while ago I thought I saw Alfonse himself, but look at me, look at me, writing to you of ghosts! It is because I am so tired almost to the point of sleeping standing up as Mr. Merriman Potts did at your birthday party, remember? I miss my children beyond any and all other concerns, I hold myself to them fatherless children now. Perhaps you might tell them I have made mistakes and I am a flawed person in the world but my love for them is not flawed in the least. I naturally refer to the love of a mother for her children. In plainest meaning I am your adoring sister who loves you—I post this in tears.

Marlais Abernathy

Epistolary intimacy can prove to be revelatory and disturbing in equal measure. Even after just three letters, I felt self-conscious to the point of worry if I wasn't myself participating in a kind of ethical transgression. I said to Mary, "I don't know if I should be reading these."

"You aren't the first," she assured me, "you're just the first from come-from-away." She meant outside of her immediate family, let alone outside of Nova Scotia. I read the next three letters straight through, as Mary sat with her eyes closed again, her hands around the cup of cooling tea.

Dearest Mary, my sweet sister,

I am writing this listing on a ship that lists terribly. I am in fever in chill and shall consider it just punishment, nor more or less than that, and as there is no apothecary on board I'll only have as medicine the admixture of sweet constant thoughts of you and my children—and the bile of everything else. The joyless posture of mind naturally results partly from my being in such tight quarters, the press of the walls and that the dark stain of murder in my heart cannot be laundered clean simply by daydreaming, as I have tried, of a childhood romp to the sea—you and I, dear sister, remember?—running to the sea, the summer roses fragrant in memory cannot rid the air below deck here of staleness. If our entire childhood should laugh at once its great amount of laughter I'm afraid it could not drown out the ringing in my ears just now, nor the corresponding harassment of pipes clanging, or something clanging against pipes as though I am in a dungeon. What comforts me, if anything does—please hold my hands in prayer—is the odd thought that surely Mr. Joseph Conrad suffered far worse weather, oh my Lord he must have ridden out gales and monsoons and other storms of Biblical proportions and intent, storms on which perhaps through the fog he saw the ghostly outline of Noah's Ark! As ever, I am afraid that just now my mind only corresponds with itself, though I see my words and touch the paper they are written on, I, who always prided herself on her cursive example. What is now most real to me my dearest sister, is knowledge that this life is not a rehearsal though at times I still believe in an afterlife—I must! Yet if there is an afterlife, I most certainly will not be in Heaven but in that Other Place for my Devil's work in Halifax against my husband, accident or not no matter. However my life even if plagued by foolish decisions of late is not to be wept over—I am aboard ship, mind and heart striking discordant bells, but still I am on my way to what I set out to do. Someone has just now called down to say New York is five possibly six hours. I slept a moment ago and what came to mind upon waking and why I do not know, the list of visiting churchwomen who traveled up from Halifax with you. Why I should recall their names is quite beyond me, but I recall a Mrs. JT White a Miss AE Silleck and Mrs. H Miles a Miss Irene Couch, a Miss Emily D. Esty, a Mrs. L Weston a Miss Ann Naudzius. All were very pleasant women as I remember them. Their names fairly flew into my head—what desperate entertainment a fever offers. The most love possible for you and my children.

Marlais Abernathy

Dearest Mary,

Please, dear one, be discrete in which details you relate to the children to give the general impression of my good health good spirits and well being and by all means do please be direct in saying that my letters do not in any way betray A FRIGHTFUL PURSUIT. At any rate, Mary, I am arrived to New York. Through Customs, what a curious inspection of body and belongings and quite unpleasant—quite. You have done this from England of course, to and back. I asked a pleasant seeming woman about lodgings, she seemed to know such things, and was advised of a place that fit my circumstances. The room has its modesty. I unpacked and folded out my few clothes bought in Halifax into a dresser drawer. I lay down and slept three hours! The wash room is down to the end of a corridor and is shared. Lying on the bed I heard children's voices from out on the street and naturally thought of mine. There is steam in the pipes for heat. I lay staring at the ceiling as I have since I was a child. Finally there was a street map to purchase. Later I was back in my room and stared out the window a long time. I am not very far from the docks, and thought My Lord, if Halifax was too much for

Alfonse how this place would have done him in! Mary, I have done something I regret and since the confessional mood has struck just now again, here is what it was: Since I do not know a soul here, I was compelled to approach a policeman and in the course of conversation told him "I wanted to be a nurse." Where oh where had that come from I shall never know. But I said it and he replied, "And where was that, ma'am?" boldly inquiring, I think, if I was a foreigner, to which I replied, "In Nova Scotia," to which he said, "In Canada, then?" naturally having a policeman's curiosity as was his nature and obligation. "And you've come to visit and see the sights?" Yes, and then I mentioned wanting to see the great Joseph Conrad and he asked, "A relative of yours?" No, no he is the author of great works to which he said Lady, I'm just an Irish cop or something close to that and do I have an address while staying in our city? When I pointed out my lodgings he said, "I'm on my way, then." Such a thing to say, that I wanted to be a nurse. I never did want that. I simply wished to tell him I'd once had a notion of usefulness of purpose, I suppose. Watching him walk away I felt small. Remember the joke Alfonse used to tell—oh I so hated it!—a man was a heavy drinker and one night he comes home and falls over in his garden, his wife dresses up in a sheet and comes out to him thinking to scare him something awful. And when this man looks up through his stupor he says Who are you? and she says I'm the Devil! "Shake hands—" he says—"I married your sister!" Now looking back I think he told that joke so often because it was about me, what he most deeply thought of me. I am not feeling perfectly well. I could use sea lilies for this cough. It always works wonders, doesn't it or teaberry and molasses. I hope it doesn't move on to pleurisy. It can, you know. That would be just punishment, being struck down by pleurisy—away from home, no serene convalescence for me, your sister. Perhaps homesickness is a real illness not just of the mind. I might well have shouted into the policeman's face I partook of a moment that killed my husband! What a fine separation from marriage I have made, what a fine example for my children! Whether he knew it or not I am the one Alfonse's joke was about. He was not a brilliant man, now, was he and not around the house enough to display fatherly talents and attentions—now that certainly is true! But his children loved him and I have helped deprive them of their father. He would not have followed me had I not left and how could it be seen more clearly than that? REMEMBER ME IN PRAYERS. REMEMBER ME IN PRAYERS, my dearest one. We will be together. I must believe the heart and what it feels is one's only true provenance, isn't it, and mine remains with you at home.

Marlais Abernathy

Dearest Mary,

Last night I had a dream about a seal-kidnapping and Alfonse was the one did it and off my children went to sea! If a dream reveals a portent what must I think? Since he is dead and buried by now, I can only think that his memory will have a stronger pull on the children than my motherhood. Sitting up weeping in bed from this dream—it had the terrible sensation of a forerunner. But Alfonse had a different fate than dying at sea, did he not, and anyway I'm only half a believer in forerunners—plus which in the dream my children did not drown. They just were towed out in a boat. Today I ventured five or six city streets to a public reading room and read that Mr. Joseph Conrad has arrived on the ship Tuscania yesterday! May 1. They call it May Day here, which you and I know to be a distress call at sea, so is one to believe that the entire nation celebrates in distress? I am certain the humor is not lost on Mr. Conrad a man of the sea, it would not be lost on him, now, would it?

I suppose had I known time and place I would have tried to greet him on the dock. I had soup for dinner on May 1. I continue to feel the pleasant freedom of the public reading room. I will continue to study the newspapers for the whereabouts of Mr. Conrad's appearance. It will be no small item! Anyway, I will find it out, I have a simple destination and must believe a simple destination can be sought and found. I washed my clothes in a basin. I am a fit sight but who knows me enough to notice. Thoughts of you and the children are what I keep closest to my person. I count my money quite often in the day. In thinking, thinking, thinking I have come to a conclusion, which is to include here my Last Will & Testament. I have never seen one actually written out so am flying in the dark with it and the thing of it is, Mary dear, I have so little to leave my children. Me and Alfonse we owned the house, the children must inherit the house and the furniture in it. Every stick of furniture every cloth every blanket and quilt every photograph in its frame every piece of knitting every hymnal and family Bibles, every item down to the Gillis lye soap. Every fond memory such as they will determine on their own. That does it, then. That is my Last Will & Testament. If I do not for whatever reason return home—go out to the stone wall in back, just where it begins to slope.

Mortimer's favorite spot to sit in the sun, just there! Dig down under the cornerstone there and do you know what you will come up with? A tin box. Look inside the tin box and you will find little clay loaves of bread. Little loaves of bread made from the sort of molding clay we used in school when we could play what we pleased. Because, Mary, you remember how at home we were not allowed to bake on Sunday! But I baked on Sunday. I snuck off and baked dozens of loaves of bread—well, that was my imagination at work! I baked and baked and many of them crumbled from dryness and so forth but some hardened nicely. Those are in the tin. I never minded religion but not to be able to pick an apple off the ground— the punishment for that!—as though baking on Sunday or eating an apple was the very thing to keep us out of Heaven when our time came! Now I've just remembered what to add to my Last Will & Testament. You remember how Mr. Matheson dressed up his scarecrows every year in October. Then arrived the year that I was ten when mother and father allowed us that visit to our cousins along the Bay of Fundy and I left my coat there! So I had to tell mother and father and they said, well, for your carelessness you'll just have to go without a coat until we somehow can send for yours. That was mostly father, I would say. Then arrived the day when I was walking along wearing double sweaters and came upon the sight of Mr. Matheson's scarecrows doing a jig. You know how Mr. Matheson was an artist at scarecrows. The one scarecrow holding a fiddle—that one had a coat on! And I just brazenly took the old coat off that one and put it on! And what's more it fit nicely! The thing a girl will do. And then father caught me with the coat when I tried to hide it. And he made me write a note of apology and deliver it along with the coat. Though he could hardly stifle a laugh Mr. Matheson spoke sternly in father's presence to me. Later at church he returned the note to me. Father didn't see this. He said keep it to remember how eloquently you owned up to something—that's a useful keepsake. Anyway, the note is amongst the pressed flowers and doily cards on the shelf in my closet. I feel you should have it. As always your loving sister.

Marlais Abernathy

Looking out the window, I saw that Mary's nephew Scott was asleep in the front seat of his truck. Mary herself was dozing in the chair. I thought how Joseph Conrad would perhaps have been quite taken by the mention of "forerunners" in Marlais's letter, and comprehended the phenomenon of forerunners with deep appreciation born of years at sea. There is a wonderful monograph, "The Folklore of Lunenburg County, Nova Scotia," written by Helen Creighton, Bulletin No. 117 in the Anthropological Series of the National Museums of Canada, which was published in 1950. Since I was collecting forerunners throughout Nova Scotia at the time I met Mary Abernathy and read her sister's letters, I had the monograph in my possession and often referred to it. Chapter 3 is titled, "Forerunners." Helen Creighton writes: "Forerunners are supernatural occurrences that announce a coming disaster."

I woke Mary up and suggested she lay on the bed, which she did. "Getting to know my sister, are you?" she said. She actually winked an eye.

I left the bedroom door open. I set her teacup in the sink, sat at the kitchen table, and took up the next letter.

Dear Mary,

What follows is an account of my famous evening last night, famous to me and no other person to be sure. When I'd gone to the public reading room I finally discovered an item in the newspaper that made my heart sink—it sank to the bottom of the sea! The column about Mr. Joseph Conrad's reading was on a kind of society page, and so I knew I would face difficulties in attending. I knew it then and there. Yet I have gone through so much, dear one, and was intent, stubborn mule that your sister is! Stubbornmost of mules! Mr. Conrad was first to appear at university here in New York where he would speak to students and then read from his work at the home of a Mrs. Curtiss James—the column said—"on the fashionable corner of Park Avenue and 67th Street." Fashionable made my heart sink but stubborn mule did walk to that address. It was hours of walking and when I arrived there was much excitement out front the home, wherein I was promptly delivered these bitter words by a doorman "invited guests only—thank you move on, now." I did protest in my best dress. I protested in the highest register of my voice. But clearly this doorman appraised me as low. I did not in fact have an invitation on my person, and how possibly could I have? I was looked upon as someone hired to bake molasses bread and bring it and be paid for it and then move on—"Move on, dear lady!" I was so tired. I felt such the immigrant, Mary. This was a world I couldn't possibly [letter smudged here] these fine and fancy [letter smudged here] and yet the characters in Mr. Conrad's stories are all common folk or most are. Later I thought perhaps it would have been best to call out to Mr. Conrad himself, should luck have it that he might hear me and see that a chair was set out. You simply cannot imagine my humiliation there, on the steps at Park Avenue and 67th street. Humiliation— quite definitely. But I do think I glimpsed the hat worn by Mr. Conrad. People moved past and around me, jostling me—I felt all collapsed. "And kindly do not wait here, madam, as the evening will run late. I don't want to have to call the police." The doorman had a nice manner about him, truth be told—he was a hireling, what else could he do? He was hired out. Should he have escorted me in saying "Of course, of course, you've come all the way from ..." was I to cost him his employment? I was not allowed in and stood across the street seeing a chandelier through the win- dow—it was the largest electric lights I'd ever seen inside a house, very impressive, dear one. To see people dressed for the fashionable evening with Mr. Conrad, to see their heads and shoulders—one man saluted another in greeting—and so there! There is my famous evening! "Where were you Mrs. Quire" my busybody desk clerk asked as I entered the small lobby, out for a walk and now I've come back, is all I could manage. Which was true enough, I suppose. My famous evening, my famous failed evening! And what a failure I am altogether I must say. You know I have dreams. At night I dream and in the dreams I remember things. That night after my failure, I dreamed about my wedding night. This is something that a woman does not talk about, but you are my sister and that is a different thing. On my wedding night Alfonse listed for me my qualities, but those qualities did not include my love of books. I should well have noted this—on a wedding night one should notice all particulars as well as impressions of a general sort. You should note what is said and not said. And now—after all that has happened to me—I am convinced that the quality left out of his list of qualities, that I loved books, is the very thing that has convulsed up from some terrible depth to smother my happiness and sense of promise. I won't blame Alfonse—no! He could not understand. I pray my children will. I had now better take a deep breath and try and come home to face whatever is waiting me, I'm sure you'll agree. All love—to my three most loved ones!

Marlais Abernathy

And what did await Marlais upon her return home? Well, she was not allowed to visit her children in their home. Instead, Mary brokered with Alfonse an arrangement wherein Marlais, Donald, and Mary could spend a day and an evening per month at Mary's home. This went on until the children were old enough to act on their own volition. Having never again left Nova Scotia, Marlais Quire died in 1957 near Guysborough.

After her "famous evening," when she returned from New York to Halifax, she had written a final letter.

Dearest Mary, dearest sister,

I am in Halifax once more. I am lodging elsewhere but The Baptist Spa. My clothes, I imagine my general appearance is to be looked upon aghast. But it is my soul feels most deeply soiled. I intend to summon up my courage here. I intend to summon it up and let whatever of it I can carry me home. My life just now feels as though it is an accident not averted. It might have been otherwise. I might have thought things through in advance and tried to educate myself in dire possibility, but I did not do that and now I am simply a woman with a woeful tale. And yet I do feel I originally left my husband Alfonse for a true good purpose, but what reason is sufficient to leave one's children? I hope to embrace you soon, dear Mary. I hope to embrace the children. And therefore I will post this letter and afterwards all efforts will go toward thinking of how to travel back. Today I looked in the mirror and wish to inform you, my sister, that I am recognizable. But my inward configuration may well have been changed by recent turmoil and vexation, worry upon worry, guilt and the general circumstances of how my marriage sorrowfully and violently came to an end. I only wish I could hide with a hymnal, oh how I wish I could be the village idiot capable of only singing hymns and doing nothing else. I would treat every day as a Sunday then! How old I feel. My one deepest question: will my children forgive me? All my love is enclosed herein.

Marlais Abernathy

I am quite often in Halifax. Sometimes I imagine Marlais Quire walking in cold fog to Halifax Harbour. I admit to keeping her photograph in my wallet.

A calendar of Nova Scotia history would inform us that in 1923 George Murray left the office of premier after serving twenty-seven years; he was succeeded by E. H. Armstrong. "Keep to the Right" was instituted on Nova Scotia highways, thereby changing from left-hand drive. Robert Chambers, eventually a famous political gadfly and caricaturist, published his first cartoon in the *Halifax Morning Chronicle.* Berwick was incorporated as a town. Mulgrave was incorporated as a town. The Sydney steel strike began—no small event, actually.

However, Marlais Quire makes no mention of events outside of her own life, except the phenomenon of Birney cars, and why should she have? She was not a tourist. She was studying the Halifax newspapers for a single purpose, to book passage to New York.

But had she been able to attend the reading by Joseph Conrad, what might she have experienced? There are in the public record two accounts. The first is from Joseph Conrad himself, in a letter to his wife, Jessie, dated May 11, 1923, which reads in part:

> And besides dearest girl, I felt at this moment (10:30 a.m.) perfectly flat, effect of reaction after last evening,—which ended only after midnight,—at Mrs. Curtiss James'. I may tell you at once that it was a most brilliant affair, and I would have given anything for you to have been there and seen all that crowd and all that splendour, the very top of the basket of the fashionable and literary circles. All last week there was desperate fighting and plotting in the New York society to get invitations. I had the lucky inspiration to refuse to accept any payment; and, my

dear, I had a perfect success. I gave a talk and pieces of a reading out of *Victory*. After the applause from the audience, which stood up when I appeared, had ceased I had a moment of positive anguish. Then I took out the watch you had given me and laid it on the table, made one mighty effort, and began to speak. That watch was the greatest comfort to me. Something of you. I timed myself by it all along. I began at 9:45 and ended exactly at 11. There was a most attentive silence, some laughs and, at the end, when I read the chapter of Lena's death, audible sniffling. Then hand-shaking with 200 people. It was a great experience.

The second account is from a woman named Eleanor Palffy, who was at the lecture and recorded:

Under the glare of electric lights hanging from the chandelier ... a man with a beard stood on the raised dais. He had the hunted look of a hare about to be strangled by a poacher. His breath came in gasps, his voice shook. Little by little the ballroom ... slipped away. This mist of sea-blue horizons blotted out.... The halting voice took on the power and assurance of its vision.... An hour passed. And then another thirty minutes. A few tired businessmen had slipped out on the points of their toes to lean in the stone doorways, muttering something about getting a cigarette, but they did not quite leave the ballroom. After all, this was the greatest writer of the English language. What a pity, though, that his pronunciations was so bad.... Good came out ringingly as "gut," and blood as "blut," which fitted in curiously with the complex beauties of his phrases.... He had been talking now for nearly two hours and a half. And so on until the end where the heroine Lena dies: capturing the very sting of death Conrad's voice broke. He was moved to sudden tears. Conrad and all who had followed him there, drunk on Conrad.

I have since read the letters of Marlais Quire hundreds of times and feel they are predominantly disquisitions on sadness and desire, preoccupied by remorse, and in a quirky way philosophical. Her style of composition, I feel, might best be described as running the gamut between chatty and a kind of Old Testament lyrical melodrama. Her run-on sentences and faulty diction aside, the fluctuating tonalities, the very atmosphere of her writing—her "style," if you will—seems to comprise a kind of symphony of influences: Conrad's prose, no doubt, hymns, the Bible, and Victorian novels, which Mary assured me Marlais read in quantity. Perhaps most poignantly evidenced by her anecdotes of childhood transgressions and her anxieties about the afterlife, she more or less characterizes her journey to New York and back as the time and place her soul has chosen to stage its agonies. Her letters, to me, sound as if they were written during held breath after held breath, with gulps of oxygen in between—she so often sounds like a woman in extremis.

In the ethical and spiritual sense, in her letters Marlais is, of course, quite hard on herself. This is a quality both endearing, because she wants to be a good person, and irksome, because she won't allow herself to savor the present moment. That is, her thoughts continually ricochet between sentimental recollection and nervous anticipation. When her letters are not outright elegiac in nature, they still seem to contain elegiac anticipation. She seems terribly often to be experiencing the foretaste of regret.

In the meantime, life is not working out for her. Yet while it is far too simple to say that all she really wanted was to see the writer Joseph Conrad read from his works, still, she did want that, and it did not happen. She merely glimpsed his bowler hat.

After I had read the letters, Mary allowed me to copy them out, which I did on Lord Nelson Hotel stationery.

She went out and spoke to her nephew, then returned to the bungalow. "One more cup of tea, eh?" she said.

Over tea, I asked Mary if she felt, generally speaking, that Marlais's daily life had been fairly typical of most women she knew. "Before my sister left home," she said, "I suppose the answer would be yes. But not for that time she journeyed out. Not then. Not then at all.

"Everyone lives with something they've done, don't they? You don't have to journey out to get yourself and everyone else all riled up, now, do you? That Marlais journeyed out set her apart, no doubt about that. She had her adventure, didn't she? The pain born of it set her apart, too, I must say. I once suggested to my sister that she read her own letters, just to see how deeply she'd been feeling things. I meant it to mean that she'd understand how her children would read the letters some day and figure out she'd done something she had to do. But Marlais never did read her own letters."

"What about Donald and Mary?" I asked.

"When Donald and Mary grew up—they live away now—they and I discussed the letters. Oh, sure, they've read them. They've read them more than once. Well, at least I know Mary has. Mary said she'd like them as a keepsake and Donald didn't protest that. But in the end she left them with me."

"Do you have any sense of how they felt about what their mother did?"

"They thought it was quite unique, what Marlais did. Either Don or Mary used that word. Oh, land's sake, I can't remember which. It was probably Mary. They didn't just scratch their heads and take it in stride, you know. In a way they had lost their mother for a time, hadn't they? You don't forget something like that, do you? No, they put some thought into who their mother was and what she did. They loved her. But there were long years they didn't get to spend much time with her. Alfonse saw to that."

"That's a sad thing," I said. "So why are you smiling just now?"

"Oh, I was just thinking about Alfonse Quire's thumb. You can't help what leaps to mind, now, can you? I was just thinking how my sister wanted so desperately to believe he was dead and buried, and all he was doing was mending a thumb. Lord, strange things go on in the world, wouldn't you say?"

CHAPTER TWO

*Love, Death, and the Sea:*
*Forerunners and Divinations*

# FORERUNNERS

IN A LETTER MARLAIS QUIRE MENTIONS A DREAM IN which a seal kidnaps her children, then reveals, "it had the sensation of a terrible forerunner."

Let me again refer to the monograph "Folklore of Lunenburg County, Nova Scotia." Helen Creighton writes, "Forerunners are known in other places as tokens or visions, but all over Nova Scotia among people of all descent, the popular name is forerunner. Occasionally they foretell happy events; more often they predict death. It is not everybody who is gifted with seeing or hearing forerunners, just as ghostly visitants are only seen by certain people. Nor do they appear only to the unlettered and uneducated folk. Certain individuals, families, or dwellings seem to be particularly sensitive to these manifestations."

During the summer of 1974, and early summer, 1975, I traveled the width and breadth of Nova Scotia, collecting forerunners and divinations, as part of a project in oral history, originally begun at and sponsored by the Folklore Institute at Indiana University, where I, a rather lackadaisical student, had obtained an M.A. in Folklore. I had some private funding, too, but used up my resources quickly, when, in a bout of acquisition fever, I purchased, at private auction in Halifax, a rare print of "Black-tailed Gannet," which Edward Lear had drawn for John Gould's *Birds of Europe.*

I didn't own a house; I had no walls on which to hang this beautiful work. But I fancied myself somewhat as a collector of natural history art, or at least aspired to that. The truth of it was, I was as much intoxicated by the tense phenomenon of auctions as anything. Anyway, I soon got in over my head. Now, no longer able to square the cost of a room at the Lord Nelson Hotel with my budget, I moved to a rooming house on Robie Street. Using this as a base, I would set out in a dilapidated two-door Ford for Cape Breton, the Annapolis Valley, and Prince Edward Island to collect forerunners and divinations. I sat in restaurants and pubs, eavesdropped incessantly and without exception was treated with kind forbearance, though far more often than not a conversation, quite understandingly, resulted in my being handed around somewhat like an annoying cousin suddenly come to visit—"Oh, you might want to go over to Antigonish and talk to so-and-so, she'd know about such things. She'd know where you might put up for the night, too."

In my experience, collecting folklore was constantly a matter of calibrating the balance between conviviality and blatant request: The people I met were generally more than willing to talk about this or that subject, but sometimes I stumbled badly and could see that the person I spoke with felt, well, "researched." This imposed an awkwardness and I backed off. Personally, I was grateful for the employment. I met lovely people I would not have otherwise met. I got to fish for salmon. I saw my first eagles in Cape Breton. I could gaze at "Black-tailed Gannet" any time I chose. Sunrises over the Atlantic were beautiful. My car was running pretty well—no small thing; the back seat was sprawled with books. I suppose it is part of the insecurity of the autodidact to write down the titles and authors of the books one has read, as if always needing to feel one is being educated. Consulting my journals, I see that in Nova Scotia that summer I had with me, *The Carrier of Ladders* by W. S. Merwin, *The Secret Agent* by Joseph Conrad, *The Brothers Karamazov* by Fyodor Dostoyevsky,

*The Quiet American* by Graham Greene, and (what had gotten into me?) a bunch of novels by Anatole France. The latter included *The Red Lily* in a compact, red leather-bound Modern Library Edition, which I had purchased in a used book store in Toronto. Why memory persists in illuminating one thing and casting another into darkness is, to say the least, a mystery. But to this day I can recall a paragraph from *The Red Lily,* and credit it as having something to do with the most private tableaux of the creative imagination: "They were dressed for dinner. In the drawing-room Miss Bell was drawing monsters suggested by those of Leonardo da Vinci. She created them in order to see what they would say, convinced that they would speak and express rare ideas in curious rhymes. Then she would listen to them. It was thus that she generally conceived her poems."

I spent untold insomniac hours writing letters and in journals, cramming as much into each day as possible. Time spent alone. During which I came to be somewhat shamefully aware that, whereas loneliness might be pitied, aloneness could be set on a higher moral plane: You could come to some knowledge of yourself. In those peripatetic months, in terms of what I deemed my potential in life—for a family of my own, for a true calling, a place to live—I can say without sentimentality that I was not lost, simply in abeyance.

What's more, I associate the summer of 1974 with discovering a central fact of my nature, that each day I have to work my way up to melancholy. Of course, it was better to realize this than to experience the effects of a quite manageable melancholia and yet not comprehend the source. A few years later in, of all places, Churchill, Manitoba, a friend, Helen Tanizaki, gave me a piece of writing by Ryunosuke Akutagawa, author of *Rashomon and Other Stories,* in which he poses the question: "What good is intelligence if you cannot discover a useful melancholy?" I have asked myself this every day since.

The same week I purchased "Black-tailed Gannet," I did research at the Historical Archive and Dalhousie University's Library in Halifax, and frequented a bakery near the Historic District along Upper Water Street and the harbor. There I met a young woman named Kristen Heckman, a student in Russian Literature and Languages at the University of California, Berkeley. She was born and raised in Nova Scotia of French Huguenot and Anabaptist German ancestry. Her ambition was to be a translator at the United Nations, which she finally became for a decade or more, then married and worked as a translator for Voice of America. The morning I met her in Halifax, I was having the first of the dozen or so cups of coffee I drank each day, when Kristen walked into the small bakery and sat down at the next table. We struck up a tentative conversation, in which she informed me that she had been taking care of her invalid aunt Tanny and that she allowed herself a midmorning and midafternoon respite, there, in the bakery. I returned that afternoon.

Kristen was quite beautiful, proved, in the short few months I was enamored of her, to be wistful, edgy, quite judgmental, with the most erotic shrug of the shoulder I have ever seen, even compared with Hedy Lamarr's brooding performance in the classic *Boom Town,* where she displayed a wonderful repertoire of shrugs and dismissive glances. Except for her red hair, Kristen very much reminded me of Hedy Lamarr. (For whatever little it's worth, I somewhat based the character of Margaret Handle in a novel, *The Bird Artist,* on Kristen, reconfiguring her complicated demeanor into a 1911 Newfoundland setting.) The directness of Kristen's flirtation was unsettling, and peculiar in that it seemed to take place only in the little bakery. When I mentioned what I was "collecting" throughout Nova Scotia, she said, "Oh, come on over. My aunt will talk your ears off about that stuff."

Her aunt lived on Robie Street, merely two blocks from my rooming house. As we cut across Citadel Park, Kristen suddenly acted as if I was "a goat who had asked her to dance" (a phrase I heard in the village of Joggins). I found this comical, she immediately picked up on her demonstration of severe formality which so contrasted with her appealing suggestion in the bakery that we "go down and look at the boats" that very evening, and she laughed a most infectious laugh.

When we reached her aunt's house, she led me directly into the kitchen, put on tea, called, "Auntie, you've got a visitor! I've already approved of him!" and, for the next hour or so, uttered scarcely more than a few sentences. Her aunt Tanny, however, was quite the chatterbox. She was, I would guess, about seventy, had been born in Lunenburg County, Nova Scotia, but in the course of her fifty-two-year marriage had lived in Meat Cove, an outport in Cape Breton, the mainland villages of Pictou and New Glascow, and "even as far away as New Brunswick for a year or two." She spoke with the slightest German accent. What she referred to as the "Devil of this arthritis" had confined her to a wheelchair, a basic model without any of the modern apparatus that enhance mobility. I looked around: The fireplace mantel and every other surface, table, desk, windowsills, were crammed with framed photographs that appeared to chronicle her family back to the nineteenth century. One round table held so many photographs that some faced in opposite directions, which was why the table was halfway out in the room: Tanny could tour her ancestry by navigating the entire circumference.

Kristen wheeled her aunt to the kitchen table. Introductions were made, Kristen served tea and cookies, then sat in the corner with an expression suggesting bemused curiosity, as if she had paid the price of a ticket and was about to be entertained. "Don't be polite to her," Kristen said, "because she won't be polite back." But Tanny was quite gracious, if a bit needling, and once I'd mentioned forerunners, she said bluntly, "I doubt you'll be able to fully understand the sort of thing you're collecting. You have to know the local circumstances and feelings, how people think."

"What do you mean," I said.

"Well, you might consider a forerunner's just a superstition. But if you live in a place where the sea has claimed a lot of people, certain ways of thinking make perfect sense."

"I've got an open mind about it," I said.

"You're from away, so you'll do the best you can, I'm sure," she said. "Let's talk a while and when we're done, I'm in for my nap. Then you and my niece here can do whatever it is you young people do when an old aunt's asleep."

She laughed; it immediately reminded me of Kristen's laugh.

As I poured more tea, Tanny said, "Is there something I don't know? In Kristen's life, are you a person of note?"

"Actually, we only met a couple of hours ago."

Kristen disappeared into another room. Then I heard the front door open and close.

"Do you intend to be a person of note?" Tanny said.

"I don't have any intentions."

"Search your heart, of course you do. What man doesn't?"

"Your niece and I just met."

"She's interesting, that one."

"That's good to know."

"Do you own a house?"

"No."

"Do you have any employment?"

"For another two months or so."

"Well, no doubt you have other qualities."

"I hope so. Do you have any idea where Kristen went?"

"My niece has probably gone out to make up her mind about you. She's soon going back to university. As for romance, her notion is, better a small fish than an empty plate."

"Well, we really just met, Kristen and I."

"In the bakery?"

"Yes."

"That's where she tends to meet all her small fish."

"Maybe I'm an act of charity."

I meant this to be funny, but Tanny quoted the scriptures: "Acts of charity cover a multitude of sins. Are you Catholic or Protestant?"

"Jewish."

"I'll be. The Hebrew faith. I'll be."

"I can leave if you're tired. I appreciate your talking to me about what I'm interested in. And anyway, Kristen brought me over without asking you ahead of time."

"Just don't hurry me, I'm not a sewing machine."

"All right."

"Let's see, where was I?" Aunt Tanny fell right asleep; Kristen never reappeared.

Predictably, late the next afternoon I went back to the bakery. Kristen came in, had a cup of coffee, then said, "Tanny's got a story for you. We'll make you supper. Want to go down and look at the ships this evening?"

"I wanted to last evening."

"What about tonight?"

"That'd be nice."

Kristen made us roast chicken and salad, set the food on the kitchen table, and promptly left the house. Tanny said, "When she's visiting me, she stays out to all hours. But I'm her only aunt still living. She gives me a lot of time. She makes a lot of effort to visit me. She stays the summer."

"We're going down to look at the ships tonight."

"Hold on to that wish."

"Anyway, it's nice of you to have supper with me."

"I wrote a note to myself," she said, taking out the note and read it. "'Tell your guest about the scarecrows.'"

"Did you tell Kristen to ask me back for supper?"

"It was my idea, yes. And she figured you'd come back to the bakery."

"Okay. Fine. What about the scarecrows, then, if you don't mind."

"I'll tell you this story, then I'm in for my nap. I'll be watching T.V. late tonight. Then later there's the radio to listen to. So I'll want to nap first, to rest up for all that."

"I'm going to write this story down. Do you mind?"

"Just don't hurry me, I'm not a sewing machine."

The scarecrows.

When Tanny was first married, she lived near Halls Harbour along the Minas Channel, which opens out to the Bay of Fundy. She had a neighbor who, as she put it, "every October set out a big family of scarecrows." Tanny could not remember the man's name, only that he kept a garden and had relatives in Vancouver whom he visited every summer, never for more than a week. "By *family*, I mean eleven scarecrows," she said, "each dressed up in clothes. Each tied to its own pole. The children loved it. It was all amusement for the neighbors, those scarecrows. The scarecrows were dressed as fishermen, they had on rain slickers, the men, the sons, and the wife and daughters were dressed in school clothes, or house clothes, just the things you wore every day. It was for Halloween, you see. It was Halloween time he'd put them out in the garden, all dressed up that way."

Then one Sunday this man and his family (wife, two daughters, one son) went to church. They always sat in the second-row pew, farthest to the left if you were facing the pulpit. It was October; the scarecrows were in the garden. When the youngest daughter, age ten or eleven, ran up the aisle ahead of everyone, she suddenly cried out, "There's a sparrow on our seat!" Or she may have called back, "There's a sparrow on our pew!"

Everyone saw that a bird had somehow got in, struck a window or the pew itself, and had died. However it happened, the bird was lying on the pew.

"Well," said Tanny, "they'd of had to have been deaf dumb and blind not to know what had just happened. The thing of it was, that day or the next, they were supposed to make a crossing by boat over to Parrsboro! But the mother—the man's wife—she was so upset, she couldn't even sit in church!

"Naturally, they did not cross to Parrsboro, but there was a drowning that very evening!

"Some young man capsized, but we didn't know him, but everyone felt that the bird had foretold it. What's more, the rest of October, and I believe on into November, the man dressed up those scarecrows in mourning. He put black clothes on them. It was as if the scarecrows were walking to church to mourn the one who drowned. Maybe this man felt the one who drowned should've been him!

"All I really remember is a sparrow got into the church and a man drowned.

"October the next year the scarecrows were back in their former clothes. The fisherman. The wife. The sons. The daughters.

"Now, you might say, 'Oh, those folks lived by omens.' But at least they knew what to take heed of. Imagine a world where you didn't!"

In eighty-eight of the ninety-nine forerunners I collected, birds were the symbol of a death foretold. (I always wondered if the fact that people knew I was a bird-watcher influenced their choices of which forerunners to tell me.) What's more, all but two of the forerunners pertained to a death at sea. I do not mean to promote the obvious as a revelation, but the latter statistic certainly seemed a clear index of how, especially in the outports of Nova Scotia, the sea, for all of its transcendent beauty, will forever maintain its reputation as a grim reaper.

"Death is part of the mystery of the sea," I heard a parson say at a funeral at Charlos Cove in 1980.

*Red at night, sailors' delight, red in morning, sailors take warning.* The sea, with its powerful temperaments of weather and fluctuating light, its ambushing furies and hypnotic lulls, its ancient painterly dialogue with the moon, its salt, its brine, floating its woven carpets of kelp, its magisterial indifference, its indecipherable secrets, its witness of human folly and courage, its evolution, its ability to migrate leviathans and transport a nearly weightless piece of driftwood thousands of miles, and always birds on its horizons, profoundly infixes itself in the literature and daily life of coastal and inland Nova Scotia.

"If you have a melancholy soul," writes Darcy McNickle in her diaries of travels in Atlantic Canada in the early 1920s, "then live by the sea, here, for it is your very nature, then, to call the sea your home."

Forerunners, it seems to me, are examples of belief naturally infused with melancholy. If one lives in a village of seafarers, drowning in general is a kind of fait accompli, and in this sense, forerunners, which verbally are equations between alertness to an omen and tragic fate, provide a code of behavior. In their basically utilitarian aesthetic, forerunners honor the seafaring life by not sentimentalizing it. It's God's grace that art is born of all of this: Throughout Nova Scotian history, folk songs, poems, short stories, oral histories, and the like have animated the sea and its perils with prodigious dedication.

I quote from the splendid short story "Devotion," by Mary McNeill-Travers: "David Cavendish asked his son out in the lobster boat, 'Do ya think you can mollify her when she's tossing us about as she now is? Stop asking me such questions and tend to your work that's right in front of ya. Do ya think, forty years at it, I care a bit to understand just now if she's joyous or in an angry rage? How should I know? And what's the difference, anyway, since we're caught in her treacherous whim and fancy no matter what? I don't think about it. I ride it out and hope to make a living.'"

One of the generosities of the Nova Scotian oral tradition is that it can illustrate a kind of magical realism, if that term is defined as a style of storytelling which plaits quotidian life with an indispensable suspension of disbelief, and which offers events of mystical or magical attributes as open secrets. But anyone who has listened to an expert raconteur knows that a passionately well-told tale, or passionately sung song, or passionately embroidered reminiscence, tells us more about *la condition humaine* than two hundred years of newspapers.

Then again, why compare? Why not just tell some forerunners? For they are also stark and unusual entertainments. These examples are without birds.

A woman told her husband that a calendar had just fallen off the wall. The husband said, "Our son's at sea, you know." The boy didn't come home.

A man had a quarrel with his brother, who worked on a lobster boat, and the brother left his house in a bad way. The brother worked all through the season, until one night, the wife of the brother was woken up and saw something moving about the bedroom. "What are you? What are you?" She ran around and took up a fireplace poker and swung it.

"What are you—get out!" It wasn't a dog with a sheet thrown over it, she knew that much. When the thing left the house, she noticed water on the floor and it was sea water, and that night the news came that her husband had drowned.

When the houses first got electricity, no one used it much, they didn't use it regularly, still preferring candles and the fireplace. But I enjoyed electric lamps. As a girl my family had three floor lamps. There were three children, me, my little brother, and my older brother. My older brother worked at sea. He fished, and he was out at sea and I got up awake very early and was about to get a fire started. I looked around and saw that two of the lamps were still on, which wasn't usual because we always made sure to turn them off at night. Two were on and one was dark. And later that morning I heard my mother crying and my father walked in with the minister of the church. I cried all through my older brother's funeral, who drowned and, what's more, they never found him.

After church I had the assignment to stack the Bibles. I was about seven or eight and I looked forward to it every Sunday. After the sermon I'd go around the pews and collect the Bibles and dust their covers and stack them up in fives. Oh, I suppose that went on for a year or more, yes, I'd say two years. They probably didn't need dusting all that much, but that was my assignment. My mother often worked at the church. She was very active with the church. Then one Sunday I was ill. I don't remember what it was, a bad cold, I think, and I stayed home from church. "Who'll stack the Bibles?" I asked my mother, and she said, "Who do you think would be good at it?" I was in bed and looked over at her and said, "I think Thomas." "Your cousin Thomas?" my mother said. And she was quite surprised, because Thomas was known as a ruffian, and to find him in church would be to find only a boy accidentally stumbled in out of the rain. "Well," my mother said, "it's you that are good at stacking books and stacking clothes after the ironing and not Thomas." "I know, but why not ask Thomas?" "All right, I'll make that suggestion that Thomas stack the Bibles, then," my mother said. And what I heard was that Thomas refused and they had to ask a number times, and finally he said all right, he'd stack the Bibles, but not if he had to attend the church service. They struck a bargain and that Sunday I stayed at home and Thomas stacked the Bibles. But he didn't stack them in fives, he stacked them higher and in a hurry. And early the next morning, the bookkeeper for the church and the minister were at a table going over the books, and suddenly three stacks of Bibles fell over. No one had taken a proper notice of how dangerously Thomas had stacked the Bibles and down they fell quite loudly, it was said. "I don't like that," the bookkeeper said, a Mrs.— I don't remember her name. She said it left a bad feeling. And the next day three fishermen drowned in a gale. It is not easily accountable, how you try to help one person and others suffer from it. There's probably a rhyme and reason but I can't tell you what it is. Maybe that minister could have.

I heard near Meat Cove three forerunners alluding to seal-kidnappings—that is, vignettes in which a seal kidnaps a child, or more rarely, an adult. I heard another one near Elmira on Prince Edward Island, two near Advocate Harbour, two near Arichat, and one at Port Joli.

Thematically, these forerunners no doubt contained echoes of age-old Scottish stories about *selkies,* or "seal people." While those may be quite varied in plot, allow me to provide a general blueprint of a selkie story. One day a fisherman—often a grieving widower—catches a seal in a net. The seal begs for her life, offering to change into a human, marry the fisherman, and bear him children. But there is one condition that must be understood: One day she might return to the sea and her own kind. The yearning for happiness (and end of loneliness) outbids the foreshadowing of loss, and the man agrees to the bargain. In certain renditions, these newlyweds attend church, raise families, and live happily ever after. More often than not, however, the seal-wife eventually transforms back into her original form; in a tragic turn of events, the fisherman (or seal hunter), now unable to distinguish his former wife from other seals, accidentally kills her, thus in effect half-orphaning his own children. One such selkie story I heard in Nova Scotia ended with the enigmatic sentence, "Forever after, the children would need be rescued from staring out to sea for a reason they did not know, and in this way, the sea owned them."

Near Sydney, Nova Scotia, in November 1977, Mrs. Hattie Gillis told me a story that contained a forerunner and yet offered a happy ending, in that no one drowned.

"I married an Australian named Devon Anderson in 1927 in Halifax, where I'd been living with my parents. He brought me up to Sydney and later to Cape Breton Island. He was in the service a while. Then he worked in the coal mines. We moved around far too much in our married life. Far too much.

"One day when we were living near Ingonish—we had a little cottage, our daughter was four years old. My husband became an accident averted. It's because he believed in forerunners, you see, and hadn't I, he might've drowned at sea. At least that's what I believe.

I don't really even care for nothin' else except to take a little credit for it.

"My neighbor, Mrs. Margaret Sperry, not too very far from Ingonish, had lost her husband. She was a widow. Soon after, or all along some say, she was a sleepwalker of the most expert sort. She had a reputation for it, sleep-walking. Famous for it, you might say. And she wouldn't simply wander about the house, no sir, she'd wander about the yard and down along the paths or the rocks, along the beach, eh? 'Oh, look, it's Margaret Sperry—there she is now! Let's lead her back to home. Come on, now, Margaret, come along home now.' You know, she never looked like she'd just jumped from sleep, either. She was dressed just as normal and nice as could be.

"One morning, still dark out, I saw her out walk-ing, and knew she was asleep. We lived next door. My husband had already gone down and joined the others. He'd found some work on a boat. He'd already gone down to join them, and up walks Mrs. Margaret Sperry. She knocked three times on my door. And I felt it right in the pit of my stomach. You hear three knocks before a death, is what I'd heard. You usually don't hear or see nothin' but the three knocks, either—you can rush to the window and not see nothin'.

"But I knew it was Mrs. Margaret Sperry deliverin' the knocks. I didn't answer the door. Instead, I went out the back and rushed down to my husband. I made such a fuss as to nearly put me in the hospital for the mad and insane! I cannot to this day even laugh about it. Not to this day!

"And the other men just told Devon to go on back home. And they went out to sea. And do you know what?—one of them fell overboard. I always felt that man replaced my Devon.

"But that man didn't drown. He was pulled back in. I'm firm in my belief that had it been Devon I'd of never seen him again. He couldn't swim a damn. You hear three knocks, a death will follow, but that time death didn't get who it first wanted. And what's more, Devon didn't disagree. We moved away from there. They were good people there and I missed them. Including Mrs. Sperry, who couldn't help herself from wandering about at night, naturally."

The archive of drownings, whether in dirge or novel, poem or tall tale, skip-rope song or ghost story (let alone police files), already seems endless, and will of course expand for as long as there is the sea and Nova Scotians living by it.

In Dartmouth, after a visit to an elementary school, I heard a skip-rope song in which a little girl drowned. I heard a tale on Prince Edward Island about a kind of sea-witch who threw a lasso of kelp around a man out in a dory, then yanked him into the dark water. At a church social near Cape Split, while telling about a drowning during his childhood, a man used a domestic metaphor to describe the sudden change in the Bay of Fundy's moods: "It was like my mother after the worst argument with my dad, how she'd pick up the end of the tablecloth and shake it all down its length, and then spend the next little while smoothing it out again."

The sea giveth, the sea taketh away. People go to sea; people drown. Then, as Swiss-born photographer Robert Frank, who lives part of each year in Cape Breton, often writes on his photographs, *Life dances on ...*


## DIVINATIONS

Divinations are an equally provocative category of belief. Most divinations that I collected basically were instructions in how to formalize a sense of possibility in the complicated realm of love. A man or woman seeking love may finally need to toss their fate to the wind, but throughout Nova Scotian history the dialectic between desire and action has obviously engendered a wonderful array of, as Mrs. Carol Moorehead, age seventy-nine, called, divinations, "love potions in words." She used that phrase while telling me not only about her own courtship, but the courtships of her two daughters and a granddaughter, "all of whom I gave advice."

*Love Potions in Words*
For a few months after she left for California, I kept in touch with Kristen Heckman through letters—or thought she was receiving my letters, that is—an attempted courtship in absentia. I exclusively wrote my letters in the lobby of the Lord Nelson Hotel on the hotel's stationery filched in large quantities during my brief residence there. I had early on subscribed to the romance of hotel lobbies, and I suppose that writing love letters in a hotel lobby only intensified it. Thinking back on their content, I recall that these letters were not examples of youthful indiscretion and erotic preoccupation. This was a stupid mistake. They should have illustrated desperate longing, whereas they merely were overly contrived in their suggestiveness. What sort of delusion, I wonder, was I sustaining? Kristen and I had kissed, at the harbor, rather at length, but that was all. What's more, she never wrote me back, which at the time allowed me to indulge in the vicissitudes of unrequited love, in and of itself an emotionally charged sort of

education. I do recall thinking of my letters definitely as "love letters," though I never actually pledged my love in them. It was more a look-into-my-soul type of thing. These letters, this engagement in an epistolary life, was, along with reading, the closest approximation to a literary apprenticeship as I was liable to obtain. Just sit in a hotel lobby and write and write and write. (Well, one has to write *somewhere.*)

To accompany all this dedication to letter writing, I also studied collections of letters in the Dalhousie University Library and in books purchased in used book stores, far fewer and farther between than exist today in Halifax, which, to my mind, has become quite a book town. In fact, I became enamored of the long tradition of letters as a public literary form, and my researches started with the ancient world. I read the philosophical and ethical disquisitions in the prodigious letter writing of Pliny the Younger, Cicero, and Seneca. I read four volumes of James Howell's letters, published in the mid 1600s, which were referred to as "intimate, chatty letters written to friends, full of observations and reflections on society and its manners"—wonderful project, I thought. In 1656 a man named Richard Flecknoe published *A Relation of Ten Years Travel in Europe, Asia, Afrique and America,* journeys related entirely in letters; from reading this I conjured up a notion of employment: I would "report back" from remote places in the world in letters to various newspapers. However, despite sending letters (on Lord Nelson Hotel stationery) to at least two hundred newspapers throughout Canada, England, Scotland, and the United States, this only panned out once. I earned $150 for a series of five letters about bird life in Atlantic Canada, published in a newspaper in Amsterdam. I heard later that the translations into Dutch were terrible. The phenomenon of epistolary nonfiction still intrigues me to this day.

Anyway, I was collecting divinations up to Cape Breton and back to Halifax, up to Prince Edward Island and back to Halifax, over to Advocate Harbour, up to Marshville, Seafoam, Toney River, and back to Halifax. Up to Port Lorne, Morden, Canada Brook, and back. And each time I returned to Halifax, I'd sit in the lobby of the Lord Nelson and write about this, that, and the other thing to Kristen, drop the letter and stamped envelope at Tanny's house. For a reason unbeknown to me, Tanny refused to give me Kristen's exact address in Berkeley, though promised to forward them.

I assumed that Tanny never read my letters. Except for one. There was one letter I asked her to read in advance of sending it to Kristen, because in it I had admitted partaking of divinations directed at Kristen. I phoned ahead, Tanny invited me right over, and we sat down for tea.

All told, in preparation for writing this letter, I had practised three divinations:

As soon as you can, buy a mirror, hold it out in front of your face, and walk backward. Stop, close your eyes as tightly as possible, open your eyes, and you will see the face of your beloved. But you have to pay close attention because the face of your beloved will quickly disappear.

Go down to the sea and wait until you see a pair of sea birds, then name them for you and whomever you want to fall in love with, or want to fall in love with you. Call out that name. If the birds don't scare and fly off, then you should have a lot of hope that things will work out. But you must do this on your own; don't bring a friend along, especially a jealous friend, and, above all, don't bring the object of your affection.

Go over to someone's home in which there is a four-poster bed, or even rent a room in an inn, then sleep in that four-poster bed. But before you fall asleep, name the bedposts. Now, either or both of two things might occur. First, you might have a restless night's sleep, and whichever bedpost your head is closest to when you awake, that is the name of the person you are likely to marry. Second, you might dream of a particular bedpost—that is, the bedpost might show up in your dream, and you'll know which one it is when you wake up.

I admitted to Tanny that, in trying out the bedpost divination, I had actually gone to a small hotel. What I didn't tell Tanny was that I loaded the dice by naming each of the four bedposts "Kristen." Anyway, I read the entire letter to Tanny and her response was, "Oh, my niece will split her sides laughing. She's not cruel, mind you, she just doesn't suffer fools."

"What do you mean?" I said.

Tanny then offered a brief disquisition on faith, provenance, and, when it came to Kristen, being realistic.

"It doesn't matter if you're from away," she said. "Some people born and raised in Nova Scotia never take to divinations or the like. It's not their way of thinking.

"My feeling has always been, it's difficult enough in this life to meet the right one, the right one for ya, and so why not open up your chances any way you can?

"Now, today, you've got young people advertising their qualities in the newspapers, what they call the 'personals,' don't they? When all that started I don't have the foggiest.

"Things such as naming bedposts? Well, what's wrong with that, I ask you? It's a hopeful tradition. It's just about hope.

"I always say to Kristen, dear, with love, don't cling to your regrets. Just move along. You have to try people out. You'll find somebody. But a prayer and a divination can't hurt now, can it?"

"Why would my letter fall so flat, then?"

"She's a modern one—bedposts, birds, mirrors, I don't think she'll suffer those. Kristen will split her sides when she reads it. Don't fret over it. It isn't everybody that can charm."

I do not particularly delight in stories whose plots rely on coincidence, nor do I feel that synchronicity is necessarily a godsend. However, I can subscribe to the Buddhist notion of predestination—surely lives meet up and all things happen for a reason, yet if the reason remains a mystery, so be it.

One bitter cold December day in 1993, I had just left the ice rink in Central Park in New York City, having skated with my five-year-old daughter. Just as the Zamboni began to erase all evidence of the zigzag, etched choreographies of skaters from the ice, I glanced over and saw Kristen Heckman helping a little boy off with his ice skates. It was clearly Kristen, nineteen years after I had last seen her at the Halifax train station, December 1974, where we had said a tearless good-bye. She now looked to be prosperously dressed, a phrase I once overheard spoken by an old Russian woman at a bar mitzvah in Halifax. On the wooden bench next to her own skates was a steaming cup of hot chocolate. I thought, Nova Scotia to California to New York, and who knows where in between: Kristen's come far in life.

"I think I know that person," I said to Emma.

"Want to say hello?" Emma said.

"It's cold, let's get back to the hotel, okay?"

"She's looking at you, Dad."

I walked over and said hello. Introductions were made, my daughter, her son, about the same age. There seemed scarcely a thing to say to each other, really. "Your daughter's beautiful," she said. "Your son's handsome," I said.

"So, you live where now?" she asked.

"Vermont," I said. "You?"

"Oh, I've lived here in New York for years. I moved here permanently in 1980."

We exchanged brief résumés, our work, what our spouses did for a living, that sort of thing. She told me that her aunt Tanny had passed away. I bought my daughter a cup of hot chocolate. Everyone had gloves, scarves, heavy overcoats on; the Zamboni was moving in concentric circles on the ice to the accompaniment of *Madame Butterfly.*

"Where in New York do you live," I said, "if you don't mind my asking."

"Near Park Avenue and 67th."

But I refrained from mentioning Joseph Conrad; it would have needed so much explanation, and to what end? "Nice neighborhood, I bet."

"My husband and I like it."

"Well, good-bye, then, Kristen."

"Funny, running into you here, of all places, huh?"

"It was a long time ago, but I always wondered why you never answered any of my letters."

"To California? I never got them."

"I sent them through Tanny. I even delivered them to her in person."

"And of course you thought she'd send them on."

"Of course."

"My aunt never did, actually. Send along your letters."

I said, "She must've had her reasons."

CHAPTER THREE

*A Birder's Notebook*

*"Shorebirds sometimes linger into October."*
—a pamphlet, "Nova Scotia," published in 1951.

## 1. The Glooskap Trail

It is one thing to sit for hours and watch a large group of Northern Shovelers at Amherst Point Migratory Bird Sanctuary along the Glooskap Trail, to be impressed and lulled by their floating, sleeping, feeding, their shifting arrays and configurations. Yet it is quite another thing to draw in close through binoculars an individual shoveler set apart in a surround of shallow salt water, to be fairly mesmerized by the sharp intelligence in its orange or yellow eyes, to note its physical attributes, the bill longer than the head, the subtle yet startling feather palette, or even catch a glimpse of its vermilion legs and feet. In other words, to have a sense of that shoveler being, as Scottish bird-artist Alexander Wilson put it, "a recluse in solitary joy, for however long it chooses to thus be a prideful hermit, therefore lavish against conformity, who will surely return to the horde and to what extent in that inevitability be given to happiness or doleful resignation, we shall never know."

I like the moment when a shoveler flies off, and if it returns, might cause a current of low-key squalling and muttering to flow through the others. Fly off, return, fly off, return, all day long, one at a time, in pairs or groups; until dusk when all the shovelers leave for—somewhere. The departure of shore birds always causes in me a sharp, melancholic pang, a gut-deep twist into a deeper emotion; light diminishes, an emptiness where moments before was such a vivid exhibition. Wilson perfectly elegizes the moment, calling out to the disappearing shapes of sea birds, "There you go, taking the day's last light and fare-thee-well, for, alas, one such as I cannot follow."

I prefer to watch birds in Nova Scotia alone, to meditate on birds only in the company of birds, and give myself over to the whims of happenstance. I do not mean to promote the obvious as a revelation, but so much of birding is happenstance. You can follow the map to Five Islands Provincial Park, Merigomish Island, Mavilette Beach, Bird Island, Chebogue Meadows, or Missaguash Marsh, to name a few proven sites (which, in my experience, are always rewarding), obsessively studied field guide in hand. But as with any investigation into the Natural World, you simply cannot account for luck. (A philosophical treatise on fate in ornithology has yet to be written.) No matter, that on any given day you either see or don't see a rail, whimbrel, sandpiper, grebe, murre, woodcock, guillemot, merganser, heron, scoter, or scaup—you are still out there in the grandeur of sea and sky, marsh or field, beach or woodland, estuary or island, and to that condition no disappointment should be attached. Landscape allows for alertness, aesthetic exactness; to paraphrase Wallace Stevens, when you look at an estuary, you have an estuary-shaped thought. Such joyful moments as when you see a particular bird you've been hoping to see are never entitlements. "Easy for tourists to see the landscape as due them for all of their hard labors in life, especially since they don't have to eke out a living in winter up here," Mrs. Elsbeth Carey, an amateur ornithologist and carver of miniature wooden birds said to me in Parrsboro, Nova Scotia, over tea at the Glooskap Restaurant.

What is it I desire by so often returning, especially in early autumn, to Spencers Beach, or Advocate Beach, or Five Islands? Naturally, it is the emotional equation between the eye and the heart: To see birds is to feel things deeply. To construct memories. Even to try and age gracefully through habits of observation. Alexander Wilson said, "As I grow older, I more look forward to seeing a bird I have yet to see, than derive pleasure from eventually seeing it, if such things such as joyful anticipation and fulfillment should even be compared."

In some thirty years of looking at birds in Nova Scotia, I had never seen a Wilson's Phalarope. Now, a Wilson's Phalarope *(Phalaropus tricolor)* is not necessarily considered the rarest of sightings in Nova Scotia, more a sighting, as ornithologist Ellen Lodge put it, "with historical overtones." That is, over the centuries of ornithological reportage by professional and lay persons alike in Nova Scotia, Wilson's Phalarope might be best termed an "accidental," quite scarcely but nonetheless possibly seen. For example, in W. Earl Godfrey's *Birds of Canada,* a book I return to as often as some might the Bible, he writes that Wilson's Phalarope "perhaps breeds rarely in southern New Brunswick (Sackville) and Nova Scotia (Amherst Point). There is a convincing sight record of ten seen off the coast of Nova Scotia, 19 June 1934 (A.O. Gross, 1937. Auk, volume 54, no. 1, p. 27); also several subsequent sight records; photo record Seal Island, 25 August 1971. Sight records only for Prince Edward Island."

I would like to add my own sight record for a Wilson's Phalarope, October 11, 2002, at approximately 7:15 a.m., offshore about thirty meters, as I stood at the wharf in Parrsboro, Nova Scotia, on the Minas Basin along the Glooskap Trail. I can effortlessly chronicle the morning's sequence. I woke up at 4 a.m., went downstairs in my bed & breakfast, made coffee, drank a cup, and filled a thermos with the rest of the pot. Took up my binoculars and meandered down to the water. Seagulls, naturally. Then I noticed at the periphery of my vision a "different" bird. The private excitement that it turned out to be a Wilson's Phalarope.

It had indeed lingered on into October. As for its identification as a Wilson's Phalarope, I have no doubt whatsoever: I checked my sighting against three field guides, photographs, and drawings. I keep no "life list," but cherish the memory of perhaps the only Wilson's Phalarope I shall ever see in Nova Scotia, or, for that matter, anywhere else.

I have most often sought out birds along the Glooskap Trail, in fact have never visited Nova Scotia—not once— without doing so. "Not the most rewarding of birding spots, I must say," Alan Ringhold, a New Zealander ornithologist specializing in geese, swans, ducks, commented when I told him my loyalty to the birding regions not in Cape Breton Island, his own preferred haunt. Birders, I've noticed, can be territorial that way.

"I beg to differ," I said, one rainy autumn day in Truro. He drove off toward Cape Breton, I toward the Minas Basin.

In broad outline, the Glooskap Trail runs from just south of Brooklyn in Colchester County, along the southeast coast of the Minas Basin, meanders north, then northeast past the Avon Spirit Shipyard, the Cheverie-Causeway Lookout, the Walton Lighthouse, dips down past the Shubenacadie River Tidal Bore, up to Truro (the "center" of Nova Scotia), then turns due west, lengthening out through Great Village, past Thomas Cove, Five Islands Provincial Park, Five Islands Lighthouse, then turns north along Route 2 until it reaches the splendid Amherst Point Migratory Bird Sanctuary, finally meeting up with the Sunrise Trail, which would take a traveler east again along the Northumberland Strait. Off the Glooskap Trail's main branch is its westward tributary, a magnificent stretch of beach and cliff all the way out to Advocate Harbour, then up along Chignecto Bay.

In Parrsboro, in a small park with a gazebo, stands a very impressive, wooden statue of Glooskap.

In an extraordinary cycle of Mi'kmaq folktales, Glooskap is forever busy adjusting and reconfiguring the topography and weather, not to mention fighting ice-giants and panther-witches, dispensing wisdom, providing outsized dramas, generally comporting himself with matchless dignity and courage, which, of course, is the essential job description of any reputable culture hero with godlike powers and an altruistic agenda. The Glooskap Trail, then, serves as an homage to Glooskap's former ubiquity and spiritual guidance, his myriad accomplishments. It also charts his historical wanderings—GLOOSKAP WAS HERE!—and any AAA map contains place-names that allude to various incidents engendered by Glooskap's arrival to this or that village, beach, cliff, lake, woodland, his interventions and triumphs, his prestidigitations and comical mishaps, even his ongoing search for a hidden cave in which to rest undetected from his mighty labors "for the rest of his days."

A number of Mi'kmaq stories are replete with birds, sometimes giant birds who cause tremendous trouble. Here is one, which basically explains WHY THE SEA WINDS ARE THE STRENGTH THEY ARE TODAY:

Glooskap liked to sit on the sand dunes and watch his Indian friends in their canoes. They were excellent paddlers and could go far out to sea. Once in a while a whale would spout, its enormous body rolling like a black wave over the sea. Its broadly fanned tail would slap down, spraying the Indians with foamy water. The canoes would rock on the swells. If one was capsized, Glooskap would right it, then pluck the Indians up from the water and set them back in, handing them the paddles.

And if Glooskap saw the dark, roiling clouds and slanting rain of a storm blowing in, he would call out, "Storm! Storm!" He would catch the jagged lightning bolts in midair. He would guide the canoes to safety.

In those days, there lived a giant, fearsome bird, whom the Indians called Wuchowsen. His name meant, "he who caused ferocious storms." Wuchowsen would sit on a boulder by the sea. Whenever he rustled his wings, clacked his beak, or scratched himself with a talon, a tremendous storm started up! He caused gales, hurricanes, lashing hailstorms that rushed in so quickly that even Glooskap had no time to warn the Indians.

One day Glooskap went to watch the Indians race in their canoes. But when he reached the sand dunes, he found many canoes washed up and splintered on the beach. One look and he knew that many Indian people had drowned. Glooskap let loose a mournful, echoing cry, "Wuchowsen, I know you have done this terrible thing!"

*A statue of Glooskap*

Just then, Glooskap saw a shadow glide over the sand. He looked up to see the grinning Wuchowsen flying past, each flap of his wings as loud as thunder.

Whoosh! Suddenly Glooskap himself was swirled up into the air by a tornado of sand. It spun him along the beach, then flung him against some boulders. This was followed by a storm that lasted for five days, and carried with it the most brutal winds Glooskap had ever known. He crouched in his cave as the wind howled outside like a thousand wolves.

"I must find that Wuchowsen!" Glooskap said. Northward along the coast, toppled trees and boulders stacked in strange formations marked the storm's trail. Glooskap followed it until he found Wuchowsen sitting on his boulder, daydreaming of storms.

"Wuchowsen!" Glooskap said with anger. "You have no mercy on people. You move your wings, clack your beak, and scratch with your talons a little too often!"

The giant bird answered, "I have lived on this Earth as long as you have, Glooskap! Storms are my life! I'll do as I please!"

But Glooskap rose up to his full size and flew high into the sky, taking Wuchowsen with him as if he were just a little duck.

Far above the clouds, Glooskap tied Wuchowsen's wings together and threw him down onto the rocks.

Now there were calm seas for many years, and the Indian people could go out in their canoes all day long without fear of being ambushed by Wuchowsen's dread storms. But gradually the water became stagnant. It grew thick and muddy. The whales fled far out to sea, where mud did not get into their blowholes, and where they could swim freely.

"We need a storm to break up these waters," Glooskap declared. "Why, I can't even paddle my magic canoe!"

Glooskap remembered Wuchowsen. "Maybe I shouldn't have been so rough on him," he said. Glooskap searched and searched and finally found Wuchowsen right where he had always lived, on his boulder by the sea. Wuchowsen's broken bones had mended and his wounds had healed. But his wings were still tied and only rustled ever so lightly, causing only a slight breeze. Only twigs were flipped into the air, only minnows were slapped to shore.

"Wuchowsen," Glooskap said, "we need your help in clearing the waters."

Glooskap approached carefully, untied one of Wuchowsen's wings—immediately a sharp wind knocked Glooskap on his back! As he lay on the ground, he heard a thunderclap and saw a pack of black clouds tumbling.

Glooskap stood up and brushed himself off. "I see you haven't lost your skills!" he said, laughing.

"Just untie my other wings," said Wuchowsen. "Then I'll brew up a storm that will last a hundred years!"

"I think not," said Glooskap. "I will keep one of your wings tied forever. Now, cause a storm that clears the water and nothing more. Or I will bind your free wing again."

Glooskap went the length of the coast in ten leaps, arriving at an Indian village. There he said, "A storm is approaching!" and as he spoke, the first squalls appeared on the horizon. Quickly, the people secured their huts. As the storm raged, they huddled inside. The thunder drummed in their ears. Their huts creaked and leaned in the wind. But all through this Glooskap stood guard, batting away jagged lightning and swallowing tidal waves.

When the weather finally cleared, the waters were running free; whales lolled about not far from shore. The sun had broken through.

The storm had scattered the Indian canoes every which way; finding each and every one, Glooskap lined them up on the beach. "Why not spend a day out at sea?" he said. And that is exactly what the Indian people did.

Every now and then, Glooskap visits the giant bird, Wuchowsen, just to make sure one wing is still bound tightly.

The Glooskap Trail, in a sense, then, demarcates the mythological opera that was Glooskap's life. For example, Five Islands—Moose, Diamond, Long, Egg, and Pinnacle—across from the village of Economy (where it is said you can "walk on the bottom of the sea" because the red sand and mud flats are laid bare at low tide) were created when Glooskap flung huge handfuls of sod at Beaver, another giant, because Beaver had mocked and doubted his magical powers. Well, Glooskap had a reputation to uphold. Now and then along the Glooskap Trail, one sees various warning signs to the effect of: always be mindful of the oncoming tide as rising tides can return as rapidly as one foot per minute. After creating the famous Bay of Fundy tides, Glooskap left them under the jurisdiction of the moon. Throughout the millennium, the advance and retreat of these tides has erased and reconfigured the coastline countless times, every day depositing tons of soil, forming alluvial plains, replenishing salt marshes, brailling the beaches with indentations of stones, dealing out clam and scallop shells like ten thousand decks of cards, leaving the mud flats glistening like various hues of black or brown shellac.

Examine a map and you will see that the Bay of Fundy almost dissects Nova Scotia from the rest of Canada. The Fundy tides are like something turbulent deep in the psyche of the planet, awesome, precarious, inimitable, let alone the province's most reliable and quite lucrative tourist attraction. The funnel shape of the Bay of Fundy collaborates with the moon in a kind of uncanny hydraulics, directing and accelerating the tide until it reaches Cobequid Bay, where, in the upper part of the bay, it may rise as high as sixteen meters. As any guidebook will tell you, this phenomenal onrush of water up into rivers and estuaries temporarily reverses their natural flow to the sea. No wonder one folklorist called Glooskap "a force of nature." In a church bazaar near Advocate Harbour, I once saw a quilt that replicated a tidal chart, the cosmic arithmetic of the tides stitched in columns, a philosophical query in flowing black cursive lettering stitched along the quilt's bottom hem: WHAT DIFFERENCE WHAT DAY THIS IS—THE TIDE IS EVERLASTING, almost as if the quiltmaker were jotting down a hymn.

ANECDOTES

Michiro Oguchi, who translated Elizabeth Bishop's poems into Japanese, sent me a sandpiper call from

Japan, made by a French company. It is a miniature pear-shaped, sepia bagpipe stitched with white thread, with two whistlelike, inch-long metal pipes. When you gently press its body, you can feel the inside stuffing, and out comes the plaintive, rusty squeak (which can echo down a beach) of a sandpiper—exactly a sandpiper's voice. I tried it along the beaches of the Glooskap Trail, with no expectation as to what the call would produce in terms of a response.

Now, I admit that, despite hours and hours of observation, I suffer Nova Scotian sandpiper-confusion, have, somewhat laughably, trouble in distinguishing the White-rumped Sandpiper from the Purple Sandpiper from the Spotted Sandpiper. The same applies to Surf Scoters, White-winged Scoters, and Black Scoters; the same applies to Greater Yellowlegs, Lesser Yellowlegs, and willets. Let's not even get into the Piping and Semipalmated Plover. On certain birding sojourns my ability to differentiate gulls (Glaucous-winged Herring, Great Black-backed, Iceland, Lesser Black-backed, Ring-billed, even Common Black-headed), especially in flight, epitomized the word "amateur." Simply put, I cannot always immediately put a name to whichever bird I am looking at, so out comes the *Peterson's, Sibley's,* or *Golden Field Guide,* and even then I often falter.

Anyway, I tried out the sandpiper call at Summerville Beach (to no effect), Driftwood Beach (the same), Spencers

Island Beach (a sandpiper flew off), Wards Brook Beach (no effect), Harrington Beach (possibly increased alertness in two sandpipers, for a moment), Carr's Brook Wharf Beach (a gull squalled at me), Saint's Rest Beach (a sandpiper flew toward me, quickly veering off), Walton Beach (no sandpipers in view), Shipyard Beach (nothing). What, anyway, would one expect from using a sandpiper call, except possibly to get some attention from a sandpiper? And then what? I believe that at each beach I was judged a fool by sandpiper or gull, and, at Spencers Beach, a crow, loon, and I think what was a Black-legged Kittiwake flying past. I take my sandpiper call everywhere.

At Five Islands Provincial Park, I inadvertently flushed a flock of dunlins out over the water, where they veered back and directly overhead gathered in a tight formation, turned and turned sharply in perfect syncopation, wings glinting like mica. This proceeded for ten or so minutes, aerial choreographies such as I had heretofore only viewed at some distance, when dunlins seemed just so much confetti on the wind. However, this close up the dunlins had weight, their creep-chit-lit, creep-chit-lit voices ricocheting in chorus off the air.

On the beach just outside Great Village, a Ring-necked Pheasant ambled from a field of stubble—odd, lovely sight, a pheasant on the beach. When it noticed me, not more than ten meters away, it did not startle up, but stood there amid puddles ("turned into shattered mirrors," poet Jane Shore wrote in a poem, "Wrong End of the Telescope," set in Nova Scotia, "long shards; blue sky and clouds lying in pieces on the ground as though the heavens had fallen down.") It was an adult female, perhaps the one I'd seen an hour or so earlier near some ditch shrubbery. It walked in what seemed fits and starts a moment or two, then flew low along the dike, then beat across a field until it disappeared into some trees. The next day I glimpsed a female pheasant in the cemetery.

I was in a sea kayak just along the Joggins fossil cliffs, when a Double-crested Cormorant "out of nowhere" flew past, close enough that I could see its green-black sheen, bright orange chin, orange-yellow eye, and precise hook of its beak, plus hear the rush of its wings. Whether stretched in flight or kink-necked atop a rock outcropping, cormorants, to me, have always been slightly eerie figures and aroused an ancient fear; perhaps it is the way they post themselves like sentinels on buoys or wharf pilings, wings outstretched, feathers splayed like a rack of black neckties drying in the wind and sun, vigilant custodians of gloom. This, of course, is utterly subjective, yet with their bony, naked throat-pouch, in their whole reptilian countenance, each time I see a cormorant I feel as though it has somehow only just then materialized out of the fossil record. My freshman zoology professor, Dr. Arvin Williams, whose tolerance for ornithological bias is at best narrow, recently admonished me for "cormorantphobia," reminding me that a cormorant's tick-grunt-croak on the nest is as much the fine-tuning of evolution as the song of any warbler, "or for that matter, your beloved kingfisher, who hardly produces arias."

Of a summer's evening on Advocate Harbour Beach, one of the best places to find driftwood in the world, I imagine, I made a driftwood fire and started to prepare some flounder in a frying pan. Gulls came by but generally kept their distance. I fried two big pieces, ate one right off with a sprinkle of parsley, sourdough bread, a bottle of beer, all the while listening to my portable shortwave radio. I remember picking up Amsterdam and, intervened by static, London and Boston. When it got dark I built up the fire, tucked inside a blanket, and, without intending to, nodded off. When I woke it was morning, the fire completely gone to ash and ember, a seagull stood in the empty frying pan, squalling, emitting raspy chirps, fluttering its wings. In the far background, gulls wheeled in the air. In the immediate background, half a dozen gulls stalked the periphery of this makeshift campsite. Now and then a gull cohort darted in, nabbed a scrap of bread, and flapped off. The gull in the frying pan merely protected its round territory, rrraaawwwkkk, rawk, rawk, raaawwwwkkk, cartoonishly turreting its head to look at me, to look at the other gulls, all of us encroachers.

Here is the Mi'kmaq explanation for the maximum depth at which loons may dive:

> One day Glooskap decided to travel to a lake not too far from the sea. When he arrived he saw a loon flying over the lake. The loon circled the lake twice, low near the shore, as if looking for something.
>
> Glooskap called out, "Loon, what are you doing? What are you looking for?"
>
> "I was looking for you!" the loon called back. "I looked for you high and low, in back of trees and in front of trees."

"What do you want?" said Glooskap.

"I will be your servant," said the loon.

"That's good," said Glooskap. Right away Glooskap taught the loon a strange echoing cry. The loon tried it out. "What is that strange echoing sound I hear?" said the loon.

"That's you," said Glooskap. "From now on, that's how you'll sound."

"How can it be coming from me and still sound as if it is coming from somewhere far off in the distance?" said the loon.

"That voice-throwing is your new skill," said Glooskap. "No other bird will sound this way."

Now Glooskap traveled around. He stopped in an Indian village. The people there were happy to see him. They gave him gifts and showed him a good time. They held a big feast. Glooskap was so pleased, he suddenly turned them all into loons! Every one of those loons became faithful to Glooskap.

In many places where Glooskap traveled, he heard Indian people say, "Oh, listen, the loon is calling for Glooskap!" or, "That bird is in need of Glooskap!" or, "Glooskap is riding out on the loon's call!" or, "There is no mistaking, Glooskap and the loon are talking with each other!"

But one day a loon, the best of divers, got stuck in some weeds at the bottom of a lake. The loon called out but could not be heard because its voice did not break the surface. The loon was stuck and soon would drown. But it happened that Glooskap was swimming there and said to himself, "It has been some time since I have heard a loon!" He listened hard—no loon. He stood by the lake, listening. No loon.

It started to thunder. "Shut up!" Glooskap said to the sky. "I'm trying to hear a loon!"

The sky said, "A loon is stuck in the bottom weeds."

Glooskap dove right down and there at the bottom he found the loon, nearly drowned, tangled up in bottom weeds. Glooskap swam up with the loon. He then let the loon fly away, and it landed near shore. The loon made its call.

Glooskap said, "From now on, you can dive almost to the bottom, but not into the weeds."

"All right," said the loon. "All right, all right, all right, I won't go into the bottom weeds, all right, all right, all right."

That is why today loons do not dive into bottom weeds. Listen closely, you may hear a loon say, "Glooskap, I didn't dive into the bottom weeds." That is what happened.

"Kingfishers have punk haircuts," my then ten-year-old daughter said. Nova Scotia has the Belted Kingfisher *(Ceryle alcyon)*, which has the signature disheveled tuft of head feathers, "combed" upward and back, the rather large head and long black beak, stout grayish-blue body with white collar. You see them around almost any body of water that has fish; I've seen a Belted Kingfisher diving into saltwater from the mast of a moored lobster boat at Whale Cove, but kingfishers, to my knowledge, rarely hunt in saltwater. If I could choose a "favorite" circumstance having to do with birds in Nova Scotia, it may well be seeing a kingfisher teaching its three offspring to hunt. I observed this near Parrsboro along the Glooskap Trail over a three-day period in 1980. I never definitely determined the nesting sight, though I think it was an excavated tunnel in a wind-eroded cutbank along a stream, because I saw both the mother and father kingfisher fly into it once. Most of each day for those three days I sat with binoculars as most frequently the mother and offspring worked from two different branches above a pond. The parent would dive along its sight line, emitting the deep crazy rattle befitting some notion of lunacy, that is a kingfisher's only call. When it nabbed a small fish, the parent carried it back to the branch, stunned it with its beak or talon, then dropped it onto the surface of the water.

Again sounding its throaty rattle, the parent encouraged the offspring to dive at the stunned fish. Naturally, this led to comical moments. Twice I observed two fledglings dive for the same fish at the same time, narrowly averting a collision, and neither managing to secure the fish. Both splashed into the water, curved back up to their excitable sibling on the branch. A kingfisher can hover over the water, rapidly beating its wings, and dive from that position. But mostly they fly straight from a branch or some other elevated spot.

The fledglings had seemed to have intuitively mastered the required motionlessness posture as they stared at the water, but as for actually catching fish, I had the distinct impression that I had witnessed only the very beginning of their education. In a notebook I jotted down that the parent-kingfishers dropped thirteen stunned fish onto the surface of the pond, whereas the fledglings were successful in plucking up merely two. Though I pride myself in the fact that kingfishers are my most beloved species, these were haphazard and unprofessional observations and data; I returned each morning merely to sit by the pond, crisp sunny mornings, warm afternoons, thermoses of coffee, cheese and tomato sandwiches, solitarily observing the age-old fishing apprenticeship of kingfishers.

Here is a Mi'kmaq story about kingfishers:

Glooskap could concoct mischief with animals and enjoyed that a lot. If he felt in the mood to make crows fly upside down, crows flew upside down and heard Glooskap's laughter upside down. If he felt in the mood to make woodpeckers knock against the bark of trees all night, just because he liked the sound, woodpeckers did that. He was proud of inventing many kinds of birds and he especially enjoyed bird-song and bird calls of all sorts. And he enjoyed playing tricks on birds, too.

When he first made kingfishers, though, Glooskap didn't come up right away with a sound this bird could make. So, the kingfishers would dive into the water and get fish and not make a sound. Kingfishers would sit on branches silently and eat the fish, but the sound of a kingfisher gulping down a fish was not a bird's song, not pleasing to Glooskap's ear.

Meanwhile Glooskap went on inventing different kinds of birds and gave each a song or call, and some sang in the morning, some sang at night, some called during the day, but the kingfishers were silent.

Then one day, Glooskap was sitting on a beach and he noticed a hollowed-out piece of wood. He put some stones in this hollowed-out piece of wood, held it to his mouth, and blew into it, and it rattled and whistled at the same time.

It was a high-pitched rattling sound—and, after blowing and whistling and rattling all day, Glooskap said, "This is the voice I will give to kingfishers!"

Before he set out to find kingfishers, though, he decided to cause some mischief with birds. He caused crows to fly upside down. He caused some woodpeckers to knock against tree bark all night. He caused seagulls to scratch his back because sand flies had bitten him. Then he set out to find kingfishers.

It was hard work, finding all of the kingfishers, and each one he found, he gave the rattling-whistle-cackle voice to. When he was done, he retreated to his cave. He fell asleep, but right away he woke to the sound of rattling-whistling below his cave. He looked out to see kingfishers flying in the air, diving for fish, sitting on branches, all making a loud rattling sound from deep in their throats.

"Maybe this was a mistake," Glooskap said. Then he decided that the kingfisher's call was all right, but not so many at once and not so many birds all together. So he made it that kingfishers kept a good distance from each other.

That is why today you usually find only one kingfisher at a pond or using a long stretch of river to fish in. You might see kingfisher families together for a while, but usually you see just one kingfisher. Or you hear it.

## 2. Garganey are Known to Wander

In my Natural History travels in the company of others, I have taken note that those of foreign extraction may come entirely undone at the sight of a rare migrant species of bird. There is a curious identification with that individual bird, or pair, perhaps been blown off course by the wind or otherwise wandered to a place foreign to its nature. I regard with astonishment and perhaps some little envy that in the sighting of such a bird a foreigner recognizes their own soul, as it were, as if the sighting has forged in man and bird, then, a single philosophy: "God shall send us where He pleases, and we shall be given, for better or worse, the experience of that."

—Rev. Eliot Fitzmorris, 1919, Halifax

Poet Robert Kelly writes, "Everything I love most happens every day." I've so often seen this or that bird, summer, winter, autumn, spring, in this or that exact same place in Nova Scotia, familiarity, never redundancy, courses in the blood. The year-round residents comprise dozens of species, of course. There are the predictable come-from-aways, who are in residence roughly spring to autumn, who nest and apprentice their young in Nova Scotia. There are the passers-through, who rest and linger along their migratory routes north and south.

Then there are the "accidentals," or, "rare migrants," those birds which happen to show up, defying their extralimital range, "blown off course," no rhyme or reason to it except Fate and Happenstance writ large. Garganey *(Anas querquedula),* for example, are not supposed to occur at all in Atlantic Canada. W. Earl Godfrey allows that Garganey are a "casual visitor" to Alberta, Manitoba, Yukon, Quebec, New Brunswick, with the proviso that "although we cannot be completely sure some of these were not escapees from captivity, the species is widely distributed in Eurasia and is known to wander."

Well, every moment of life contains paradox, does it not? I saw a Garganey off the coast of Meat Cove, Cape Breton Island, Nova Scotia. I was with two crack ornithologists who saw it, too. Godfrey writes of the male Garganey (the one we saw was indeed a male), "Body size and bluish upper wing coverts suggest Blue-winged or Cinnamon teals, but the blue is paler and more grayish. Adult male (except in eclipse plumage) is readily separable by a conspicuous white narrow curved area extending from above the eye to the nape, by lack of white crescent in front of the eye, and by sharp contrast between dark breast and white belly. In both sexes the gray, instead of yellowish, legs of the Garganey distinguish it from Blue-winged and Cinnamon teals." Indeed, it was seeing the Garganey take flight and noting its gray legs that first alerted us to the possibility that it was not a teal. Mary Parker, who had done field work in Europe and Asia, had an inkling: "You know, it kind of reminds me of a Garganey."

"If that's true," Michael Caplin said, "then that bird's way out of town, isn't it?" Within a longer journal entry all I could allow myself was, "Beautiful, clear day. Watched unknown sea duck for at least twenty minutes."

Years later in 1994 I published a novel, *The Bird Artist,* set in Newfoundland and Nova Scotia, in which the protagonist, Fabian Vas, sights and sketches a Garganey.

In January 1999 I received a letter from a Mr. Alan Clarke, which in part read, "The likelihood of your character seeing a Garganey is far-fetched, though I suppose not impossible. But how would he even know to call it a Garganey? You don't mention that he had access to a field guide or monograph of any sort in his small Newfoundland village that would supply such a reference, allowing him to recognize the species he drew.

*Garganey at rest*

Besides, why import from another continent when there are in the very pages of your novel you have so many species native to the waters of the province that eventually became Newfoundland and Nova Scotia?" I scarcely mind this sort of letter, full of odd scrutinizing and complaint, opinion and even disappointment in that an author hasn't got things quite right.

I took this letter to Halifax, the Haliburton House Inn on Morris Street, my preferred place of residence in that city. There I wrote Mr. Clarke, suggesting that rather than a Garganey "importing an arbitrary eccentricity" (his phrase) into the story of murder, a love-triangle, and art, it was merely an opportunity for young Fabian Vas to test his artistic flexibility, i.e., drawing any bird requires certain perceptions and skills. My complete response, five handwritten pages, now that I think about it, was no doubt a stifling disquisition on literary imagination. To his credit, Mr. Clarke wrote me a second letter, quite autobiographical in tone, which summerizes his own research into the distribution of Garganey, and furthermore addresses the issue of artistic license: "Your reply has helped me to understand *The Bird Artist* and why you chose the Garganey for its metaphoric role. I respect your comment on verification vs verisimilitude. Is that what separates artists, word or otherwise, from lawyers? (Anything that separates real people from lawyers is worthwhile!)"

For the purposes of depositing much of it in a university collection, my friend Olivia Tecosky organized and cataloged my manuscripts, diaries, photographs, letters, translations, tapes, linguistic anecdotes, folktales, bird lists, drafts of novels, notebooks of all stripes, a good amount derived from travels and extended stays throughout subarctic, Arctic, and Atlantic Canada, roughly from 1969 to 2000. In this process Olivia dug up a file called "Garganey Correspondence" (sounds rather like a title by Robert Ludlum). This file contained 111 letters between myself and sixteen different correspondents in five different countries. The nature of the letters I received can, for the most part, be defined as passionate, knowledgeable, at times insufferable in their didacticism or quite wacky in their obsessions. Each of them featured the Garganey. While the level of scholarship and sharpness of insight greatly varies, these are letters from people truly looking at the world and thinking about birds, thus re-reading them was a heartening reward.

Yet, of course, personality was in evidence. Allow me one example (August 27, 1988) from a letter sent from Scotland by a fellow just returned from a birding sojourn in Cape Breton Island, Nova Scotia. After delineating in great detail the circumstances surrounding his own three sightings of a Garganey in Europe, he adds, "Congratulations on the birth of your daughter. John Creighton, whom I met in Mabou, informed me. You perhaps remember John. He sends his best. Now, for the truly important things in life! On my initial all-day trek along the highlands, I saw—." He proceeded with a litany of sea birds, just their names, nothing else.

I dashed off a letter stating, "Reading your account of European Garganeys—and now those Cape Breton birds—I was happily envious for you. Some day I'll bring my daughter up there and show her some places you probably haven't discovered yet. You have to know the right people, of course." Naturally, the phrase "happily envious" contains opposing sentiments; I blame my persnickety tone on what I took as the competitive atmosphere of his letter, least which the subtle implication that the fabric of my memory was full of holes—the truth was, I had traveled in ornithologist John Creighton's company throughout an Arctic archipelago, shared hours of conversation. John has three daughters.

As for "Garganey Correspondence," it occurred to me that the phenomenon of seeing a bird that has wandered an especially impressive distance from its normal range can be quite a haunting thing. It certainly makes one think about Time and Distance and Wanderlust. It seems as if one can glean from seeing a "migrant" a sense of the origin of wandering on Earth, what Bruce Chatwin called the "oldest peregrinations." I cannot quite articulate this, it has an elusive quality. Perhaps it has something to do with investing hope and trust in the fact that the world is not completely discovered, that true, unforeseen mysteries are continually played out by wild creatures. That when some anarchy quickens in their little brains against the more predictable insistences of evolution, birds may travel to places they are not supposed to travel to, and therefore "lavish against conformity."

"What I especially love about your seeing a Garganey in Nova Scotia," Patricia Langhorn wrote in a letter in 1996, in response to a brief article in which I mentioned my odd good fortune, "is that such sightings are so democratic. I mean, anyone might have seen it, been in the right place at the right time, don't you think?"

I do indeed. And then there was this, in a letter from Penelope Frances Oliphant, a sixty-six-year-old professional gardener, who filled the margins of her two letters in 1996 with expertly drawn hummingbirds: "My husband and I went on our honeymoon to Maine, Nova Scotia, and New Brunswick in 1946, just after the war. Looking out at the sea rocks and crashing waves of Cape Breton, the sky that summer often brooding up a squall, a very restless and mischievous sky, we felt, we absolutely delighted in the sheer amount of bird life to be seen. And no matter what Science may insist as being true of where birds are supposed to live, I can only imagine what sailors and fishermen, who no doubt know birds without necessarily knowing their Latin names, had seen across the centuries! Why, a Garganey off the coast of Nova Scotia may be the least of it!"

Such a letter, of course, is not a vindication, since vindication is not desired. It simply underscored the fact that the Garganey I saw was an exhilarating presence and gift.

The scientific vocabulary of ornithology is put to best use in exquisite writing such as Peter Matthiessen's

*Wind Birds,* which is a celebration of his home and birding haunt, Long Island, especially the wetlands, potato fields, and beaches immediately around Sagaponack. With incomparable deftness, Matthiessen poeticizes scientific vocabulary by plaiting it into brilliantly evocative descriptions. Indeed, the vast archive of natural history writing in libraries around the world puts a good face on Homo sapiens for posterity—we have paid attention and celebrated our planet, when otherwise so much of our relationship with nature, needless to say, has been and continues to be dismally species-centric and rapacious. (In October 2002 the ornithologists I spoke with were terribly disturbed by obvious evidence of global warming throughout Atlantic Canada.)

There is a kind of found poetry in even the driest monograph, such as the one I recently read, "Parasites in the order Anseriforms (Screamers, Swans, Ducks and Geese)"—simply because a reader needs to pronounce the resonant names of birds themselves. In Nova Scotia, the categories of birds are COMMON IN SUITABLE HABITAT, FAIRLY COMMON, UNCOMMON, SELDOM SEEN, AND "ACCIDENTALS."

COMMON IN SUITABLE HABITAT and FAIRLY COMMON: Red-throated Loon, Common Loon, Pied-billed Grebe, Horned Grebe, Red-necked Grebe, Northern Fulmar, Cory's Shearwater, Greater Shearwater, Sooty

Shearwater, Manx Shearwater, Wilson's Storm-Petrel, Leache's Storm-Petrel, Northern Gannet, Great Cormorant, Double-crested Cormorant, American Bittern, Least Bittern, Great Blue Heron, Louisiana Heron, Black-crowned Night-Heron, Yellow-crowned Night-Heron, Glossy Ibis, Snow Goose, Brant, Canada Goose, Wood Duck, Green-winged Teal, Northern Shoveler, Gadwall, Eurasian Wigeon, American Wigeon, Canvasback, Redhead, Ring-necked Duck, Greater Scaup, Lesser Scaup, Common Eider, Harlequin Duck, Oldsquaw, Black Scoter, Surf Scoter, White-winged Scoter, Common Goldeneye, Barrow's Goldeneye, Bufflehead, Hooded Merganser, Common Merganser, Red-breasted Merganser, Ruddy Duck, Turkey Vulture, Osprey, Bald Eagle, Northern Harrier, Sharp-shinned Hawk, Cooper's Hawk, Northern Goshawk, Red-shouldered Hawk, Broad-winged Hawk, Red-tailed Hawk, Rough-legged Hawk, Golden Eagle, American Kestrel, Merlin, Peregrine Falcon, Gyrfalcon, Gray Partridge, Ring-necked Pheasant, Spruce Grouse, Ruffed Grouse, Yellow Rail, Clapper Rail, Virginia Rail, Sora, Common Moorhen, American Coot, Black-bellied Plover, Lesser Golden Plover, Semipalmated Plover, Piping Plover, Killdeer, Greater Yellowlegs, Lesser Yellowlegs, Solitary Sandpiper, Willet, Spotted Sandpiper, Upland Sandpiper, Whimbrel, Hudsonian Godwit, Ruddy Turnstone, Red Knot, Sanderling,

Semipalmated Sandpiper, Least Sandpiper, White-rumped Sandpiper, Baird's Sandpiper, Pectoral Sandpiper, Purple Sandpiper, Dunlin, Stilt Sandpiper, Buff-breasted Sandpiper, Ruff, Short-billed Dowitcher, Long-billed Dowitcher, Common Snipe, American Woodcock, Wilson's Phalarope, Red-necked Phalarope, Red Phalarope, Pomarine Jaeger, Parasitic Jaeger, Long-tailed Jaeger, Great Skua, South Polar Skua, Laughing Gull, Black-headed Gull, Bonaparte's Gull, Mew Gull, Ring-billed Gull, Herring Gull, Iceland Gull, Lesser Black-backed Gull, Glaucous Gull, Great Black-backed Gull, Black-legged Kittiwake, Sabine's Gull, Ivory Gull, Caspian Tern, Roseate Tern, Common Tern, Arctic Tern, Forster's Tern, Black Tern, Dovekie, Common Murre, Thick-billed Murre, Razorbill, Black Guillemot, Atlantic Puffin, Mourning Dove, Rock Dove, Black-billed Cuckoo, Great Horned Owl, Snowy Owl, Barred Owl, Long-eared Owl, Short-eared Owl, Boreal Owl, Northern Saw-whet Owl, Common Nighthawk, Whip-poor-will, Chimney Swift, Ruby-throated Hummingbird, Belted Kingfisher, Red-headed Woodpecker, Red-bellied Woodpecker, Yellow-bellied Sapsucker, Downy Woodpecker, Hairy Woodpecker, Three-toed Woodpecker, Black-backed Woodpecker, Common Flicker, Pileated Woodpecker, Olive-sided Flycatcher, Eastern Wood-Pewee, Yellow-bellied Flycatcher, Alder Flycatcher, Least Flycatcher, Eastern

Phoebe, Great Crested Flycatcher, Western Kingbird, Eastern Kingbird, Horned Lark, Purple Martin, Tree Swallow, Rough-winged Swallow, Bank Swallow, Cliff Swallow, Barn Swallow, Gray Jay, American Crow, Common Raven, Black-capped Chickadee, Boreal Chickadee, Red-breasted Nuthatch, White-breasted Nuthatch, Brown Creeper, House Wren, Winter Wren, Marsh Wren, Golden-crowned Kinglet, Ruby-crowned Kinglet, Blue-grey Gnatcatcher, Eastern Bluebird, Veery, Gray-cheeked Thrush, Swainson's Thrush, Hermit Thrush, Wood Thrush, American Robin, Gray Catbird, Northern Mockingbird, Brown Thrasher, Water Pipit, Bohemian Waxwing, Northern Shrike, European Starling, White-eyed Vireo, Solitary Vireo, Blue-winged Warbler, Tennessee Warbler, Orange-crowned Warbler, Nashville Warbler, Northern Warbler, Yellow Warbler, Chestnut-sided Warbler, Magnolia Warbler, Cape May Warbler, Black-throated Blue Warbler, Pine Warbler, Prairie Warbler, Palm Warbler, Bay-breasted Warbler, Blackpoll Warbler, Black-and-White Warbler, American Redstart, Prothonotory Warbler, Ovenbird, Northern Waterthrush, Connecticut Warbler, Mourning Warbler, Common Yellowthroat, Hooded Warbler, Wilson's Warbler, Canada Warbler, Yellow-breasted Chat, Summer Tanager, Scarlet Tanager, Northern Cardinal, Rose-breasted Grosbeak, Indigo Bunting, Dickcissel,

Rufous-sided Towhee, Tree Sparrow, Chipping Sparrow, Clay-colored Sparrow, Field Sparrow, Vesper Sparrow, Lark Sparrow, Savannah Sparrow, Ipswich Sparrow, Grasshopper Sparrow, Sharp-tailed Sparrow, Seaside Sparrow, Fox Sparrow, Lincoln's Sparrow, Swamp Sparrow, White-throated Sparrow, White-crowned Sparrow, Evening Grosbeak, Dark-eyed Junco, Lapland Longspur, Snow Bunting, Bobolink, Red-winged Blackbird, Rusty Blackbird, Common Grackle, Brown-headed Cowbird, Orchard Oriole, Northern Oriole, Pine Grosbeak, Purple Finch, Red Crossbill, White-winged Crossbill, Common Redpoll, Pine Siskin, American Goldfinch, House Sparrow.

Uncommon, Seldom Seen, and "Accidentals":
Pacific Loon, White-tailed Tropicbird, American White Pelican, Brown Pelican, Magnificent Frigatebird, Tundra Swan, Greater White-fronted Goose, Barnacle Goose, Willow Ptarmigan, Purple Gallinule, Sandhill Crane, Northern Lapwing, Wilson's Plover, American Avocet, Eskimo Curlew, Marbled Godwit, Curlew Sandpiper, Franklin's Gull, Little Gull, Gull-billed Tern, Royal Tern, Least Tern, Sooty Tern, White-winged Dove, Barn Owl, Northern Hawk Owl, Chucks-will's-Widow, Say's Phoebe, Scissor-tailed Flycatcher, Cave Swallow, Carolina Wren, Sedge Wren,

Northern Wheatear, Varied Thrush, Loggerhead Shrike, Golden-winged Warbler, Black-throated Gray Warbler, Townsend's Warbler, Cerulean Warbler, Worm-eating Warbler, Louisiana Waterthrush, Kentucky Warbler, Black-headed Grosbeak, Lark Bunting, Chestnut-collared Longspur, Brewer's Blackbird, Hoary Redpoll, Wild Turkey,

and—thank you very much—Garganey.

CHAPTER FOUR

*Driving Miss Barry*

ON JULY 7, 2002, MY WIFE, JANE, DAUGHTER, EMMA, her friend Millan, and I boarded the *Cat,* a catamaran transporting tourists from Bar Harbor, Maine, to Yarmouth, Nova Scotia. Rocky seas predicted, I bought Dramamine in the gift shop. Half an hour at sea, though the horizon was bright with a kind of watercolor wash of white, rains lashed the windows. On a video screen the ferry's route was chronicled with a dotted line across a map of Atlantic Canada. It reminded me of the way black-and-white movies depicted time passing: Sometimes a ten-day passage in dangerous WWII submarine waters took ten seconds of a dotted line urgent as Morse code on the screen. As I stood out on the back deck and watched the nearly phosphorescent alluvial fan of water from the huge propeller, felt and heard the slightly disturbing basso continuo whine and growl of the engine, I read "The Sandpiper," a poem by Elizabeth Bishop, one of the great poets of the twentieth century. She was born in Worchester, Massachusetts, in 1911. Her childhood was peripatetic. After her father's death, she moved with her mother to Great Village, Nova Scotia, along the Bay of Fundy. From April 1915 into 1917 they lived with Elizabeth's paternal grandparents in a house that was transported from the village of Mount Pleasant in the 1860s. Elizabeth returned to Great Village each summer from 1919 to 1930.

> *The tide is higher or lower. He couldn't tell you which.*
> *His beak is focused; he is preoccupied.*

from "The Sandpiper"

"Preoccupied," naturally, alludes to the singular condition of the writer, the beak a pen, the entire stanza the mental weather of composition. In terms of such symbolism, my understanding is too ... *obvious,* isn't it? Too simplistic, my assertion that to survive, artists (like the sandpiper who works the boundary between land and sea) must reside at the margins between the practical and the infinite in order to best meditate on the conditions of existence.

Still, the poem "The Sandpiper" does indeed have much symbolic overlay. The sandpiper is a small creature and yet, by its proximity to the sea, we associate it with eternity.

The poet observes the sandpiper in the moment, and yet the poem itself, its reliance on forms and sensation, like all great art, offers a way to resist short-lived reality.

In *Becoming a Poet,* David Kalstone writes of "The Sandpiper": "The bird, on the one hand, is battered and baffled by the waves; ... on the other hand, it attends and stares, is preoccupied, obsessed with the grains of sand, a litany of whose colors, minutely distinguished, ends the poem.... Bishop lets us know that every detail is a boundary, not a Blakean microcosm. Because of the limits they suggest, details vibrate with a meaning beyond mere physical presence. Landscapes meant to sound detached are really inner landscapes. They show an effort at reconstituting the world as if it were in danger of being continually lost."

On the deck of the *Cat* I laughed, remembering an ornithology monograph from the early 1900s having to do with northern California, in which the ornithologist equated a stretch of beach to the margins of a page in a book: "The sandpipers, dunlins, sanderlings and others lightly impressed the wet hieroglyphs of their footprints as marginalia."

That "The Sandpiper" is my favorite of Elizabeth Bishop's poems is, no doubt, a naïve and (to poets, let alone scholars of her work) transparent choice, predictable for someone as preoccupied with birds as I am. Still, it is my favorite. Elizabeth Bishop observes a sandpiper; in Nova Scotia, it might be a Purple Sandpiper, a Spotted Sandpiper, a White-rumped Sandpiper. Yet, since Elizabeth Bishop spent so many years in Brazil, it is most likely *Actitis macularia (Linnaeus)*, the Spotted Sandpiper, whose winter range includes Brazil. But what I love most about "The Sandpiper" is its physical momentum, how its imagery in turn agitates and soothes the heart. The tide comes in, the tide goes out; a sandpiper stitches zigzag along the beach, say near Great Village, Nova Scotia, "looking for something ... Poor bird, he is obsessed."

In the Haliburton House Inn on Morris Street, Halifax, I met on the morning of July 8 with a woman dutifully and brilliantly "obsessed," in her inventive scholarship and writings about Elizabeth Bishop. She is Sandra Barry, who has written *Lifting Yesterday,* a diligent, idiosyncratic, exhaustive 490-page study of Bishop in Great Village, of the village itself. Sandra may know (though she would protest this) more about

Great Village than anyone alive. Self-deprecatingly, Sandra says of her book, "It's more than anyone wants or needs to know." I disagree; it is a vital addition to Bishop studies and, what's more, a corrective to certain previous writings, as well as a lens through which to view the early part of the twentieth century in Nova Scotia.

"Bishop writes beautifully about birds," I said, over breakfast of coffee, cereal, and fruit, the morning buffet in Haliburton House Inn.

"I've often thought she writes about them ecstatically," Sandra said. "Like St. John Perse."

"I know I'm speaking too literally here, but from an ornithological perspective, in 'The Sandpiper,' she gets a thing or two wrong."

"'As he runs, he stares at the dragging grains,'" Sandra said. "Yes, you mentioned that line."

"Only in the sense that no sandpiper really stares at anything; they don't pause, certainly not to meditate. They just hurry along."

"The argument would be, it's Bishop's projection, of course. It's her own persona she locates inside the sandpiper's, her own *nature,*" Sandra said. "To stare. To scrutinize. To make connections. Plus, she calls the sandpiper 'a student of Blake,' remember? Well, of course it's Bishop herself's a student of Blake! It's quite funny, really. To me at least. The poem has humor, doesn't it."

"I liked that this particular sandpiper is 'in a state of controlled panic.'"

"You identify with that, do you?" Sandra said, chuckling. "Well, I suppose I can, too. And think of EB herself. That she might've imagined herself inside a nervous, flitting sandpiper. Oh, my. That might be quite exhausting, don't you think? Possibly quite enthralling, too."

"A poet includes only what she has to in a poem. Yet Bishop doesn't include a certain fact—that the sandpiper's just looking for something to eat! That's what they do all day!"

"Now"—laughing—"there you really *are* being too literal! Still, poets do have to eat, they have to make a living, don't they? There's a lot going on in that poem."

Sandra has what my old aunt Helen called an honest laugh. She finished her tea, I finished my coffee. Talking, talking, talking about Elizabeth Bishop with Sandra Barry. Quite an education for me. Her etiquette in the face of my ignorance was more than generous. She navigated around any and all unschooled queries, or deftly revised them, all for the sake of spirited conversation.

July 9. The Haliburton House Inn is the only place I now stay in Halifax. I placed much of my noir novel

about murder and spirit-photographs, *The Haunting of L.,* there. This morning I woke at five a.m., went next door to the main building, and sat in the library/sitting room. The small lobby and dining room were empty. I moved to another chair, then the sofa, and a word of Scots-Irish derivation, *mallalorking,* came to mind. It roughly means "restlessness before a journey."

I first came across the word in a Newfoundland-English dictionary, and have heard it used twice in actual speech. The first was at the ferry launch in Yarmouth. A quite elderly woman, reprimanding her daughter with a smile and shake of her head, said, "Can't you stop your children's mallalorking so damn impolitely?" The grandson had opened a suitcase and tossed a shoe into the sea.

The second time was on a train from Halifax to Vancouver, the TransCanada route. I was sharing face-to seats with an elderly gentleman from Edinburgh. As we passed a stand of oak trees along a river—I think we were in Quebec—he pointed out to me a man and woman kissing in the shade of a tree. "I was a military surgeon thirty years," he said. "I took in a lot of first-hand medical knowledge, you see. But ..."—he nodded toward the amorous couple—"there's no cure for *that,* now, is there, those mallalorking hearts and all. But don't be fooled, the young don't have a patent on it, now, do they?" He took out a flask of whiskey and I gladly accepted a swig.

Restless, then, wanting to get on the road to Great Village, I read yesterday's newspaper, waiting for breakfast.

Out the window I could see thick fog over Halifax Harbour. Finally, the staff set out pitchers of orange juice, thermoses of coffee, muffins, fruits, cereals, milk. I had been duly warned by my travel companions not to wake them, nor to telephone Sandra Barry at some ungodly hour. I was not to hurry people. I sat at a corner table drinking coffee and reading today's paper.

There was a heading: "Smoke Haze Expected to Blanket Province." The article began, "Most Nova Scotians will likely wake up in a haze this morning as smoke drifts over the province from forest fires burning in northern Quebec. 'A haze of smoke had already crept up on Yarmouth and the Nova Scotia-New Brunswick border by Monday afternoon,' said David Mason of the Maritime Weather Centre. 'The smoke was expected to move eastward overnight and blanket the province by this morning,' Mr. Mason said Monday evening."

There was another heading: "Titanic Spirit Voices, Come In, Please." It turned out that a professional psychic medium named Alan Hatfield, from Pictou Landing, had spent the previous morning trying to record voices of some victims of the *Titanic* disaster in the Fairview Lawn Cemetery. At one point Mr. Hatfield claimed to detect a spirit saying, "The time is right." "I know we have lots of cooperative voices today," Mr. Hatfield said.

My travel companions come in for breakfast around seven-thirty; Jane, Millan, Emma, and Sandra Barry, who has walked down from her apartment carrying a small travel bag.

I load the car while they eat breakfast. We sit around till nine. As previously discussed, throughout the journey, woven into the conversation will be an ongoing Q & A concerning Sandra's life and work. I already was quite aware of her accomplishments as an archivist, poet, historian, but soon learned of her natural kindness, her ability to size up and adapt to a naturally shifting domestic mood inside a crowded car.

A few years ago, Jane, who had known and worked with Elizabeth Bishop in the 1970s at Harvard, had given a lecture at the Elizabeth Bishop Conference in Wolfville, and visited Great Village with Sandra Barry. They were already friends. Over the past weeks I'd been reading several years worth of Elizabeth Bishop Society newsletters, each a small anthology of criticism, disquisition, poetry, photographs. I had also read Sandra's piece "The Art of Remembering," in Volume II, Number 1, of the *Nova Scotia Historical Review.* In addition, in *Collected Prose,* I'd read Bishop's own reminiscence, "Primer Class," and stories, "Memories of Uncle Neddy," and perhaps her most well-known prose, "In The Village."

And I'd read the poems obviously set in Nova Scotia, the astonishing "The Moose," as well as "Sestina," "Filling Station," "Poem," "First Death In Nova Scotia," a few commentaries about each, and Lorrie Goldensohn's highly regarded *Elizabeth Bishop: A Biography of a Poetry.* That is to say, I was just beginning to comprehend who this great poet was and the breadth of her accomplishment. I already knew of the centrality of Bishop's work to my wife and, obviously, to Sandra Barry.

In the car we listened to a cassette of Elizabeth Bishop reading her poems. Jane and Sandra laughed appreciatively at certain inflections and nuances that completely escaped me. In fact, dozens of references to Bishop's life and writing went over my head. They had a shared Bishop "vocabulary," is how I thought of it. Meanwhile, Emma and Millan piped in with comments and intelligent questions, in between chatting, taking photographs out the windows, listening to CDs, as the car breezed along the Bay of Fundy.

From the start, however, my primary interest was in Sandra Barry. Who is she, this utterly unique woman my old aunt Helen would have complimented to her face, "You're certainly an odd duck, now, aren't you?" How had she come to Elizabeth Bishop in the first place? How had Sandra applied her own meticulous intelligence to bringing a small Nova Scotia village— Great Village—to readers with such vivid immediacy? How does she carry on, without even the basic sinecure of academic affiliation, or at best unpredictable support of any kind? I do not mean to suggest that I fancy Sandra as some sort of nineteenth-century scholar "throwback," an archivist-monk scratching letters with a quill pen by candlelight (an enterprise she might prefer, actually), who can scarcely manage modern life. I only mean to say that why her passion and knowledge about Bishop's childhood years sustains her, probably has some correspondence to how Sandra relates to her own childhood in the Annapolis Valley of Nova Scotia. In speaking with her, I wanted to develop, to some extent, a portrait of a freelance scholar, as Sandra herself put it ironically, "a somewhat marginalized occupation in a somewhat marginalized place."

"I should just hire you to give me a series of lectures about Bishop's early life," I said in the car.

"Oh, no," Sandra said, "this is much more fun."

After merely a few exchanges, what came to mind was yet another of my aunt Helen's oft-used phrases, one meant to illustrate a certain generosity: "Her head was fairly brimming with news." For in touring us through early twentieth-century Nova Scotia, I felt that Sandra, to quote Chekhov, was a "subtle practicioner of the anecdote." She divvied out anecdotes of local history with a sense of almost gossipy anticipation, as if all we needed to do was speed up the car a little and we'd catch up with and witness the event she had begun to tell us about.

"Oh, stop right here!" she said, for instance, as we drove through and past Great Village. "This is probably the exact point where Elizabeth got on the bus. You know, for her bus journey through New Brunswick down to Boston, the one she writes about in 'The Moose.'" We all stared at the weedy edge of the road, as if deciphering the pressed image of Elizabeth Bishop's shoes in the tamped dirt.

Turning the car around, driving again through Great Village and past Elizabeth Bishop's childhood home across from the gas station, we finally pulled up at the Blakie House, a sprawling Queen Anne Victorian. Standing next to the car, we looked out toward the Minas Basin. The sun backlit a hazy general thickness of cloud. There were also ribbons of smoke like jet trails on the horizon. "Definitely that's from the Quebec fires," Sandra said. "It's been like this for a number of days now."

As it happened, we were among the first customers the new owners, Sarah Peterson and Michael Burnett, had at the Blakie House, located at 8 Wharf Road, Great Village, Nova Scotia. On the back of each of the traveler's cards stacked on a table in the side hallway, it read OF

INTEREST IN THE VILLAGE, listing "Eastern Bore; Elizabeth Bishop's Cottage and four other Provincial Heritage Sights; Layton General Store; Lowland Gardens; Strawberry U-Pick (In Season); Smith Holdings Antique; World's Highest Tides—viewing all along the Fundy Shore."

Naturally, Sandra knew the entire history of the Blakie House and got the owners quite up to speed on it.

After unloading suitcases, cameras, notebooks, my travel companions settled into their upstairs rooms, then began a tour of the house. I set out on a walk to the Minas Basin. The dirt road wound over a small bridge, then along an open field. Almost immediately I saw two juvenile bald eagles patrolling the creek. Later, when I mentioned these birds to Sandra, I was touched by how preoccupied she was with keeping to her job as tour guide. "Oh, I'm sure EB saw eagles whenever she walked down to the water."

"Now, Sandra, remember it's you I'm most interested in. You, the biographer. Have *you* often seen eagles here?"

Sandra looked at me askance, then realigned my priorities in a patient, professional tone. "Yes, I'm quite certain young Elizabeth would've seen eagles. She had the keenest eye."

Anyway, I continued on for half a mile or so to the long dike, then climbed it for a view of the Bay of Fundy. The water was roiling muddy red-brown, with half a dozen eddies twenty or so meters offshore, as if sea monsters were about to surface. There was a nipping wind. A lone sandpiper hustled along a thin stretch of beach. It looked to be stitching up the border between land and sea. Again, a phrase from Chekhov came to mind: "In the girl's school there was an emergency seamstress always at the ready."

That evening after dinner at Blakie House, we sat in the parlor, with its high ceiling, scrolled mantel, piano, while Emma read from a book of Nova Scotian ghost stories. She put on her best eerie voice, finessed certain passages melodramatically. The story, as one of its sentences read, "caught the fright nicely." However, Millan seemed skeptical, unable to credit the story, and was dubious about everyone else's suspension of disbelief, or let us say susceptibility to belief in specters. "Am I the only one here who *doesn't* believe in ghosts?" she said. Millan and Emma were at the time fourteen.

"I think so," Sandra said. "But who knows? Maybe something will happen on this trip to change your mind."

We all nervously laughed. A look of only slightly eroded skepticism, yet one not entirely absent of possibility and intrigue, crossed Millan's face. Emma noticed this and seemed pleased. They're great pals, intuitively perceptive about each other's quirks, curiosities, affections.

I stayed up until four a.m. quoting Sandra Barry in my moleskin notebooks.

On the morning of July 10 at about 6:45, Sandra padded downstairs and found me in the library of the Blakie House. "Sleep well?" I asked.

"Yes, very," she said. "Very comfortable room. The most benevolent of ghosts, too."

"Oh, good."

"I see you have coffee."

"Yes, there's some in the kitchen."

It was, perhaps, too early for formal conversation, but when Sandra sat down in the leather chair, I took out my notebook, and she looked resigned and willing. "Sandra," I said, "where were you raised, where'd you go to school, were there any particularly beloved books?"

"Oh, my."

"Sorry, I seem to have been up most of the night waiting for you, I suppose."

"Not at all. Let's jump right in. Well, let's see. I was born in Middleton, Nova Scotia, known as 'The Heart of the Valley.' That's the Annapolis Valley, of course. When I was three, my parents moved us down the road a few miles to Bridgetown, known as 'The Friendly Town.' I did my own primer class at Bridgetown Elementary School."

"Did you experience your primer class anything like Bishop did hers?"

"Not in exact detail, of course, no, but in general atmosphere, the ambience of rural Nova Scotia primer classes, yes. When I read her story 'Primer Class,' a lot came back to me from my own experience in school. What's more, we moved to a nearby village called Paradise, and I did my grade one in Paradise School, which was very much like the Great Village schoolhouse, actually somewhat smaller. Then we moved back to Bridgetown, and from grade two to grade twelve I attended Bridgetown Elementary and Bridgetown High Schools. The high school had about four hundred students."

"To your mind, is homesickness locatable within a general sense of nostalgia in Bishop's writings?"

"There's certainly much painful memory in her work. I realized that all over again when I read the collection of her letters, *One Art.* During her time in Great Village she did suffer a few actual illnesses. She was confined to bed for periods of time, kept out of school for various periods.

"In her letters she expresses a kind of fond longing for Nova Scotia, and it's there, too, in the poetry. In certain letters her nostalgia, if you will, for Nova Scotia is bolder, more exact. And, yes, I'd say painful. Now and then she expresses an urgent desire to visit Atlantic Canada. Something—childhood?—seems almost to summon her, though that sounds too mystical. A sad summoning, yet sometimes a happy one, too, for certain aspects of childhood, for life in general in a small village, Great Village."

After breakfast at the Blakie House, Sandra said, "Shall we go see Elizabeth's house?" But as it happened, Emma, Millan, and I set out on foot, while Sandra and Jane stayed at the table to talk.

Earlier in the summer, Emma had participated in a rigorous two-week residency at the Maine Photographic Workshops in Rockport, Maine, working exclusively in black-and-white photography. She took her camera everywhere. I had asked her to chronicle our trip, that is, to take photographs on request, as well as according to her own interests. Within a few minutes' walk we arrived at the Great Village schoolhouse. Emma took photographs from across the road, the parking lot, closer yet. At that hour of the morning, much to our surprise, there was a steady traffic of trucks, including logging trucks, "out and back from Truro," as one store-keep put it. Great Village is obviously set along a route of local and provincial commerce.

Perhaps writer John Berger is correct, photographs are quotations, they cannot possibly recapitulate the entire narrative of a place. But they can evoke certain prototypes of experience. Sizing up the Great Village schoolhouse, Emma remarked, "Take away the phone wires and maybe that new truck, it's hard to tell what year it is. It's like I can almost see myself going to this school when Elizabeth Bishop did." And that seemed right. The schoolhouse did engender what Berger called a "historical empathy." The architecture had a timeless feel. The schoolhouse itself retains a utilitarian intimacy, quite a different thing from quaintness.

"Me, too," said Millan. "Maybe we say that because everybody's talking so much about Elizabeth Bishop when she was a child."

In her article "The Art of Remembering," Sandra writes:

> Her "Canadian schooling" had not been extensive, but the experience left a more positive mark on Bishop and formed the basis of one of her most delightful prose reminiscences, "Primer Class." Bishop attended the Great Village School during fall-winter 1916-17, although for some of that time she was ill. "Primer Class" is a wonderful evocation of the fascinations and trepidations of a child experiencing her first formal schooling. The Great Village School, still standing and in use, was an impressive structure to her young mind: "The school (Bishop wrote) was high, bare and white clapboard, dark red roofed, and the four-sided cupola had white louvers."
>
> Perhaps one of the most important and lasting experiences from this time was her introduction to geography: "Only the third and fourth grades studied geography. On their side of the room, were two

*The Great Village schoolhouse*

rolled-up maps, one of Canada and one of the whole world. When they had a geography lesson, Miss Morash pulled down one or both of these maps, like window shades. They were on cloth, very limp, with a shiny surface, and in pale colors—tan, pink, yellow and green—surrounded by the blue that was the ocean. On the world map, all of Canada was pink; on the Canadian, the provinces were different colors. I was so taken with the pull-down maps that I wanted to snap them up, and pull them down again, and touch all the countries and provinces with my own hands."

"Elizabeth Bishop loved maps, you know," said Sandra later that day. "And just think of some of her titles, 'North and South,' 'Questions of Travel,' 'Geography III.'"

⚜

Joined at the schoolhouse, then, by Sandra and Jane, we all walked to the house itself. On the way, Millan and Emma, as if manifesting a predisposition toward intense nostalgia themselves, reminisced about certain of their grade-school teachers. These were hilarious, poignant, replete with vitriol, deep affection, detail. "I remember how Miss — was already in a bad mood by the time school started." "I had this one teacher who thought she was such a fashion plate!" "I loved Miss —, she made us happy." "My fifth grade teacher was evil." The adults exchanged glances; naturally, we ached to tell our own stories.

Sitting on the side porch of the house, I asked Sandra what it was like first visiting Great Village.

"When my friends first took me to Great Village," she said, "that fall day in 1990, I felt a synergism, I suppose, because so many levels were working at once. I connected deeply with Elizabeth Bishop's art, the fact that Great Village is a beautiful spot, the fact that I was experiencing, though it was by no means simple, a direct link between art and life."

"So, each time you return, all that's felt again, intensified, added to?" I asked.

"Yes, it's a visceral experience for me. I feel physically grounded when I come here. Again, its connected to childhood. Where I grew up in the Annapolis Valley, we were only a few minutes' drive from the Bay of Fundy. While I had problems feeling connected to Bridgetown, I always felt something intrinsically real about the universe when I was standing at the edge of the Bay of Fundy. This is my most direct connection to landscape. In turn, when I saw the part of the bay around Great Village, I was stunned. It felt even more like the place I belonged than even the places I was raised."

Sandra had a key to the house. Stepping into the kitchen was like stepping into one's own reading, let alone an earlier time. The owner, a friend of Sandra's, was not at home. The house felt very much lived in, not museum-like in the least, though it is dedicated to Elizabeth Bishop's memory and work and more or less open to the public by appointment. We signed the guest book, perused the literature on a small table: scholarly articles (including Sandra's), Elizabeth Bishop's books, several photographs of the house at various times in the twentieth century. On the wall of the sitting room was a particularly haunting photograph of a baptism, in an icy lake or stream. Standers-by are wearing thick coats, scarves, boots, gloves. "Talk about coming awake to the Lord!" Sandra quipped. "More like *startling* awake to the Lord!"

Sandra is the best possible tour guide. She provided us with the house's architectural history, pointed out objects referenced in Bishop's writings, all delivered in an informal yet respectful manner. On the second floor, which somehow felt crowded with rooms, we stood in front of Elizabeth's room.

It is startlingly small. Emma was drawn to a pair of scissors locking closed the slant window, and took several photographs of it. She then took still lifes in other rooms, the tops of bureaus, mirrors, other compositions and tableaux.

As we stood in the largest bedroom, Sandra sighed deeply. "This, of course, is where the scream took place," she said. "This is where Elizabeth's mother cried out. She was having her nervous breakdown, and some time after was sent to hospital. And Elizabeth never saw her again."

This statement, for all its biographical compression, seemed largely for Millan's and Emma's benefit, as if to say, *Things were difficult in this house and it's best to say it directly.*

"You might remember, Emma," Sandra said, "Elizabeth's story 'In The Village' begins, 'A scream, the echo of a scream, hangs over that Nova Scotia village.'"

*Sandra Barry on the front porch of Elizabeth Bishop's childhood home*

"Amazing story," Emma said, "—and it could freak you out if you let it. But it's very cool being in this house. But kind of sad, too."

"Well," Sandra said, "the room we're standing in is where that sentence is derived from."

The actual, physical location from which a sentence is "derived" makes an impression. Besides which, I happened to be holding a copy of *Collected Prose* and read the second paragraph of "In The Village:"

> She stood in the large front bedroom with sloping walls on either side, papered in wide white and dim-gold stripes. Later it was she who gave the scream.

"Sometimes—and it's simply my inclination, I suppose," Sandra said, "I associate the story of Elizabeth's mother with a kind of Victorian tale, of family, of madness, silence, absence, things spoken of and not spoken of. But one shouldn't romanticize it. It was all so painful. It always strikes me as so, I don't know, *generous,* just how much actual detail Elizabeth gives us in her stories."

We visit the first-floor rooms again. In the sitting room, I tell Sandra that when Jane and I had stopped by this house in 1984, we had seen a copy of the *New Yorker* containing "In The Village" on a table. "Do you recall first reading it?" I had asked Hazel, Elizabeth's distant cousin by marriage, then living in the house. Her answer struck me then, and later to an even greater extent, as epitomizing rural Nova Scotian social restraint, all the while acknowledging the fundamental unpredictability of life.

"Well, you see," Hazel had said, "it's all true, everything Elizabeth wrote. It's beautifully written, of course." She paused to stare at the magazine, then out the window. "I've never understood, though, how Elizabeth could tell so many strangers what happened here."

Later, Jane and I speculated on whether Hazel had even an inkling of just how many "strangers" had, over the years, read "In The Village."

"Oh, but I suppose that's what great writers do," Hazel continued.

On the walk to the Blakie House, we didn't speak for a while, then I asked Sandra how, to her mind, she was perceived in Great Village.

"I trust I'm perceived as someone who cares deeply about the village," she said. "I've always advocated that the work of the Elizabeth Bishop Society needs to remain centered here, that the village is the nexus, in a way, in our efforts to honor her life and work. I suppose those in the village who know me regard me favorably because I'm not really from away. I don't think people view me as any sort of professional; that is, I'm viewed differently from academics.

"I would hope that Great Village folks view me kindly. I would be grateful for that. The people who know me always seem glad to see me when I visit. Probably some view me as a kind of caretaker of Elizabeth Bishop's legacy, in a local sort of way. And that suits me just fine."

Later the same day I walked to the small post office and mailed two letters, one placed inside a tin candy box I'd purchased in the general store. Standing in the post office, I thought about what Chekhov, master chronicler of village life, wrote of one of his characters: "The beautiful and uneasy privilege of visiting the house of such a sullen and joyful childhood, both usual and unusual for the times, where certain inhabitants, the ones that should be in someone's diary, seemed to have the deepest heart, the deepest soul, the deepest observance of time simply by their natural inclinations." Through Sandra's portrait of her, I felt this about Elizabeth Bishop in her childhood.

In a certain, selfish regard, I had wanted to sit all night in the kitchen of Elizabeth Bishop's house, candles lit, conversation between Jane and Sandra a kind of séance, bringing Miss Bishop into the present. Millan and Emma and I would observe from a corner, or sitting on the stairs. On the other hand, I had experienced a disquieting sense of trespass in the house, much more difficult, at least for me, to articulate. Partly it had to do with the fact that Sandra's and Jane's knowledge of Bishop's life seemed more appropriately well-met with the privilege of setting foot in the house itself, a house I could best relate to only impressionistically. Partly, too, it had to do with the haunting power of Bishop's own writing, especially the story "In The Village." We had read the story aloud in the car, and then, later, had stood in the room in which the scream had sounded; all of this reminded me of Bishop's own thought: "Life and memory of it so compressed they've turned into each other. Which is which?"

I suddenly did not wish to know more "facts" about Bishop's life. No more anecdotes. Not for a while, at least.

I simply wanted to time-travel, to have lived in Great Village at the beginning of the century, to erase all vicariousness and replace it with quotidian life. It was a feeling (as so often happens in my life) of nostalgia for a time and place I never experienced. No doubt, too, given our age of terrorism, the agitated density of daily existence, resident in that nostalgia was a precise longing for peace-of-mind, early twentieth-century sea air to breathe, the ability to breathe it calmly and collect one's thoughts.

Yet the life of Elizabeth Bishop insistently disallows sentimentality. Because, in the very least, we know her childhood in Great Village contained its severities, along with what Emma called, "just normal kid stuff, like long walks to go swimming."

"Yes," Hazel had said on our visit in 1984 (I had written it down and kept it all of these years), "Elizabeth wrote beautifully about such painful things, didn't she. If you don't feel things deeply as a child, and see things clearly, you could never write like that later on. Oh, I'm sure of that."

The next day we drove to Parrsboro and bought sandwiches at a bakery. We had a picnic in the shade of a gazebo near the wooden statue of the giant Mi'kmaq culture hero, Glooskap, in a small park at the intersection of two roads. Jane and Sandra spoke about Elizabeth Bishop's letters; an eavesdropper might be convinced that they'd indeed memorized all five hundred letters in *One Art*. These dozens of epistolary relationships, working in concert between the covers of a book, provide as powerful an autobiography as could be expected; an astonishing collection, really.

After lunch we drove the winding coastal road to Advocate Harbour. I was hoping to find the house I'd lived in in the late 1970s, when it was loaned to me by playwright Sam Shepard. I hadn't been back to Advocate Harbour in many years. One does not necessarily expect any landscape in Nova Scotia to change much at all. "The upkeep is a bit more impressive," is all I could come up with when we entered the vicinity of the house. The area had been turned into a well-kept park, with a railinged path down to the beach, and it took a while to recognize the big house on the hill.

"That's got to be it," Emma said. "There's no other house around. Dad, just walk up and if somebody's home, tell them you used to live there."

Sound advice, neither too presumptuous nor allowing the regret of not having tried. I walked up the long dirt driveway. When I reached the house, I saw that it was being wonderfully renovated. There were stacks of plywood in the yard. Three men, each holding a hammer, stopped to look over. I waved. Two of the carpenters went directly back to work. The third, however, walked across the yard. "Sorry to bother you," I said, "but I used to live here."

The carpenter, a handsome fellow in what I took to be his late thirties, or very early forties, turned out to be co-owner, with his wife, of the house. "I'm Stuart," he said. We shook hands. "Howard Norman," I said. "I lived here in the late seventies."

"A friend of Sam's, then—did you ever own the place?"

"No, stayed here is all."

"Well, come on up. My wife Megan's inside. She'll want to meet you."

"I've got a bunch of people with me. My family and two friends. Is it okay if I get them? I've been telling them about this house for years."

"We'll get you something to eat."

I walked back to the car, gathered everyone, and we all walked back to the house. By this time Megan had come out onto the lawn. Introductions were made. When Stuart and Megan turned and started back to the house, I noticed a somewhat strange expression cross Sandra's face. She whispered something to Emma, who in turn whispered something to Millan. I could not for the life of me figure this out.

We toured the house. I showed everyone my "old" room on the second floor, which was being painted.

Emma took photographs of the piano downstairs, the same piano that had been in the house when I lived there. Megan and Stuart were splendid hosts, on an obviously busy day. They took us through each room, saying what had been done to shore it up, what personal touches they'd added, and so on. Clearly, it was going to be a beautiful, dignified house; even amid the disarray it already felt like a family lived a rich, full life in it.

"I heard some pretty famous people came out to visit here, back in the seventies," Stuart said.

"I think so," I said. "Sam was already pretty famous. But he kept a low profile up here. That's my understanding, at least. It was one of the great gifts of my life, this house, no matter how brief a time I stayed in it. It's like that Neil Young song, 'All my changes were there.'"

"I know what you mean," Stuart said. "It's a good place to think things through."

Addresses and telephone numbers were exchanged. Stuart said, "I've put our Los Angeles address on that piece of paper, too. I stay here through lobster season. That's one of my jobs. In the winter we're in Los Angeles, mostly." Mention of Los Angeles seemed at best enigmatic, but I had long ago ceased having any presumptions about how, where, and why people lived where they did. Anyway, there had been, in just that hour's time, a flood of memories. It was a very pleasant visit.

In the car, on the road back to Great Village, Sandra looked at Emma and said, "Can you believe it?"

Jane and I still were clueless. "Believe what?" I said.

"Dad," said Emma, with dramatic exasperation, clearly shared by Millan and, more mercifully, by Sandra, "that was Megan Follows. She was Anne of Green Gables! God, you're really out of it!"

"The most famous actress in all of Canada, I should imagine," Sandra said. "Anne of Green Gables is how she's first and even best known, but she's had many remarkable roles since. Many. She's quite brilliant."

"Do you think Elizabeth Bishop ever read *Anne of Green Gables?*" Millan said.

After four days on Cape Breton Island, we returned to Halifax. On our last evening together this time around, I still had some questions for Sandra Barry, both pertaining specifically to her reading of Elizabeth Bishop and herself, as well.

In the library/sitting room, tape recorder on the table, I said, "What was your earliest reading of Elizabeth Bishop? For that matter, Sandra, what was the progress of your thinking that led to such a dedicated project, your book, *Lifting Yesterday?*"

"It begins, really, in 1988," Sandra said. "But there's

a preamble. My love of historical fiction and nonfiction led me to two degrees in Canadian history, a B.A. and M.A. at Acadian University and the University of New Brunswick. When I completed these degrees, I was at sixes and sevens about what to do with my life. I wanted to be a scholar and writer, but just didn't know how to do that. Rather than grab the bull by the horns, I retreated back to university. In the fall of 1987, I returned to the University of New Brunswick to do a qualifying year for a creative writing M.A. One of the courses during the winter term was 'American Poets Between the Wars,' a seminar taught by Robert Cockburn.

"The assignment in class was to give a presentation on one of four poets, Robert Lowell, James Dickey, James Wright, or Elizabeth Bishop. I went to the bookstore and bought the texts, which included Bishop's *Collected Poems 1927-79*. But before I cracked the cover, I went to the library and took out *Collected Prose*. The very first thing I read was 'Primer Class.' And as I read the memoir of her early life, I felt as though I was reading my own experience, or at least something very akin to it. I know we've spoken of this, Howard, but there it is again. I thought, 'Oh, Elizabeth Bishop is not really an American. She's a Maritimer.' I say Maritimer instead of Nova Scotian, because it speaks more to geography and landscape, rather than a geopolitical entity. What happened to me in that little academic setting, that literature course, was, for the first time in my life, where I connected art and artist at the most profound level I could manage.

"Now, I realize that there's nothing especially unusual about any of this—in the wide world, I mean. Many people have such moments. However, it was unusual in my life. Elizabeth Bishop's work, reading it, studying it, writing about it, all of it has marked a profound change for me."

At breakfast, tea and sweet breads, slices of melon, coffee, I said to Sandra, "I hate to leave, really. I always hate to leave Nova Scotia. I really hate it."

"I'm sad to see all of you go," she said.

"It's been fun, hasn't it?"

"Great fun."

"How's your life here in Halifax, your working life and so on? Do you mind me asking? It's just so I can think about it on the ferry back to the States."

"Well, I have a pretty simple life here in Halifax," Sandra said. "Partly, it's because of financial restraints, my meager resources, you know. But also it's because it's my nature to keep things low-key, I think. Organized and uncluttered. I do my work. I do a lot of reading and writing. I spend a lot of time in solitude. Sometimes I think of Elizabeth Bishop's question in one of her letters, something like, 'Do you think the Great Village house would be a good place to retire in my old age?' I apply the question to myself, only substituting the Annapolis Valley."

"So, then, Sandra," I said, "the real question of travel would be where you wish to retire, to live out your days?"

"Yes. I enjoy life here in Halifax. But somehow I expect that I shouldn't end up in the city. My old age should take place in a village."

EPILOGUE

*Robert Frank
Equals Late Autumn*

Late October. 6:00 a.m. In my hostel
room near Mabou,
when the pre-set radio "wake up"
came on (a Chopin nocturne).
I had been dreaming of Robert Frank's photograph
"The Mail Box at the Road to Findlay Point, Mabou,
Cape Breton, Nova Scotia, Fall 1976."
(In the dream the photograph was a billboard,
the sea behind it.)
This photograph fairly defines
what Picasso called
"the reality of dreams in art,"

that is, a perfectly composed visual duet
between the unconscious and conscious mind.
It looks like a "painted" photograph;
in fact it is signed by both Robert Frank and his wife,
painter June Leaf,
who added brushstrokes.
The photograph evokes a dawn or dusk-lit
fog besotted smoky ocher hue.
A road gently curves left to right along a headland.
Except for an unbroken stretch
of sky across the top, the photograph
consists of seven adjacent panels,
each slightly aslant, and was taken
with a Polaroid Instamatic camera.
The road moves us through time
left to right. However, the panel
at the far right, the seventh panel,
abruptly alters the perspective,
because it squares a view straight on out,
which depicts a car (or is it a small truck?)
trundling along toward a different headland.
One way to interpret this is that the car
has just made the sharpest possible
left turn at a three-way stop.
If the driver is meant to be
the photographer himself,
(the drive along the coast being his specific memory),

symbolically and literally he is exiting his subject.
The vehicle's back lights, twin opaque red circles,
seem to be mutely flaring.
You can almost feel the heat cranked up
inside, the drizzly chill of the air.
You can almost hear, on the dashboard radio,
Otis Redding's rough-hewn plaintive,
"… it's raining in my heart."
Such dreams of observing—
or living "inside"—Robert Frank's
Cape Breton photographs have,
over the years, recurred quite frequently,
nights in a row sometimes:
a gazetteer of my sleeping hours,
whenever I sleep in Cape Breton.
Of this particular photograph, Christoph Ribbat,
in the book *Hold Still–Keep Going,*
writes, "… we owe it to Robert Frank's works on Nova
Scotia that nature was given a different visual language.
In clear distinction to the exacting
professional landscape photographers,
he doesn't treat nature
as a space in need of aesthetic domination.
Instead, he shows it as an uncertain
dreamlike sphere of memory."

Born in Zurich, Switzerland, in 1924 to Jewish parents, Frank came to maturity during World War II. While his mother was Swiss, Frank, like his father, was a German citizen. Although relatively safe and prosperous, the family lived in fear that Hitler might invade Switzerland. (Frank became a Swiss citizen in 1945, shortly before the end of the war.) This early experience undoubtedly contributed to Frank's tendency to observe society from a distance.

7:00 a.m. After coffee and buttered toast,
I was actually driving my dilapidated Datsun pick-up
through what I call "Robert Frank Territory."
I continued on out along a similar headland
in quite similar misty light
as in "The Mail Box at the Road to Findlay Point,"
my windshield absorbing
the exact same hue.
On the front seat, the map drawn for me
by the hostel's proprietor.
Actually, she had drawn an insert map in pencil,
on the official map I had purchased at the gas station.
Anyway, there I was
meandering toward Finlay Point.
For years now, this is how it has been;

on late autumn visits to Cape Breton—in my mind
I have to work my way through
certain of Robert Frank's photographs
in order to catch up to the present.
Is this a form of life imitating art?
I don't know and don't care, really.
The mental process now seems inevitable;
and I suppose I have come to value it
like no other.

12:30 p.m. Lunch in Red Shoes pub
in Mabou (which displays pairs of red
shoes in the window). On a napkin
I wrote a few of Robert Frank's
melancholic aphorisms
which he sometimes scrawls
on his photographs: *"Hold still—keep going,"*
*"Life dances on …,"*
*"Look out for hope,"*
born, it seems to me, of sorrow and hope,
grief and reprieve from grief.
It is a biographical fact that Mr. Frank
and his first wife, Mary,
lost two children, daughter Andrea in a plane accident
and son Pablo, a different path he took.

It is a cosmically stupid
assertion that "time heals all"
(it is the opposite of wisdom),
it heals some things,
but a certain kind of experience
exacts more pain as time passes
simply because it has become
so full (and tenaciously) resident
in one's heart and mind.
Robert Frank has made nearly unbearable—
and singularly incomparable—
photographs containing the oldest,
most fundamental human paradox,
deepest joy and deepest sadness,
within a single frame.

In 1970, after separating from Mary Frank, Robert
Frank bought a house in Mabou, Nova Scotia, with
the artist June Leaf. The raw, strong work he made
there was, is, a demonstration of how far a photograph
can stretch, how much it can include, once it gives up
the idea of including it all, once it accepts that it isn't
going to break on through to some universal truth.

Salman Rushdie
*The Ground Beneath Her Feet*

&#x269C;

1 p.m. I drove from Mabou to Whale Cove.
Wind high. White caps.
("White horses on the sea,"
as they say.)
The horseshoe-shaped beach. The rock jetty.
The wharf gulls vigilant
toward the fishing schedule.
They sight the boats
and gather en masse
for handouts.
In September 1975, I lived a few weeks
in Whale Cove while trying to recover
from walking pneumonia.
Since childhood I have been susceptible
to respiratory attacks of every stripe,
and in Whale Cove my coughing
in the few neighboring restaurants
and churches I frequented
soon became legend.
My lungs ambushed with knifing spasms.
It must have been alarming to witness.
I was the village's coughing freak. (It was
entirely understandable, but nonetheless
humiliating, to have a child come out and ask me
to leave church premises,

a disturber of the peace,
even though I'd merely stopped by to admire
the oratory prowess of the minister, had
in fact stood outside listening in through a
slightly opened window.)
All sorts of home remedies were suggested;
I tried some to good effect.
Dressed in winter bundling,
I took a walk each morning,
got exhausted in a few minutes,
sat on a patch of beach grass, wheezing,
dozing off, back against the wind-sculpted sand cliff,
like a beached walrus
taking in the sun.
I "took the waters"
only by looking at the cold sea.

2 p.m. I sat in a small
shop/restaurant, a few scattered tables,
actually, in Whale Cove,
and thought about the 1975 photograph
"Andrea,"
by Robert Frank,
which has much writing on it,
and a portrait of Andrea

in its upper-left panel,
who has the most naturally stunning smile.
Read left to right, the next panel
suddenly evokes, if you will,
landscape without daughter,
and the entire nine-paneled work
suggests how the mind in turn
illuminates and blanks,
because four of the panels
contain grainy emptiness.
That second panel scripts a piercing
epitaph, "for my daughter Andrea who died in
an Airplane crash in TICAL in Guatemala
on Dec. 23. Last year. She was 21 and she lived
in this house and I think of Andrea every DAY."
The house is depicted in the centermost panel
and again in the last panel, lower right
in the photograph.

Frank continued to experiment with multiple
images, adding objects, notes, and scraps of paper
to achieve a sense of intimacy in structure, form,
and content.... In one of his most impassioned
statements, Frank roughly pasted several images
on cardboard, adding layers of black, peeling paint,

obscuring and defacing the overall picture. It was
as if he was using the surface of the photograph as
a palette on which to inscribe his pain.

Philip Brookman

*Robert Frank: Moving Out*

3:30 p.m. I drove to Chimney Corner
and again sat by the sea.
A seal bobbed up its head, observed me,
swam a ways to my left, dove, surfaced again;
it went like that for half an hour.
Gulls, of course. Thermos of coffee.
It appeared as if half the horizon
was filled with rain clouds, the other half empty.
A block of gray-black, a block of blue. The
gray-black working surprisingly fast to the right,
meshing into the blue.
Wet chill wind.
(Once, on a beach on Prince Edward Island,
an ornithologist
friend and I stood right where the rain ended.
It has to end somewhere, naturally;
it just was the oddest thing, for a few moments to be
able to reside at that exact margin, step in and out of
the rain at whim, like walking through a curtain.)

In cinematic narration,
as in literature, a "flashback,"
of course, delays Time,
doubles Time's presence,
folds the past into the present.
Robert Frank sets up frames within frames.
This on occasion has the effect of a "flashback."
The frames also isolate parts of a landscape,
as if particular emotions—or memories—reside there.
Sitting at Chimney Corner, I closed my eyes
and envisioned Robert Frank's winter collage
constructed in Mabou, 1979, I think simply titled
"Mabou." It consists of six panels.
Each panel displays an upright wooden frame.
The first panel (read left to right), shot from below
the house, has a big wooden frame
inside of which is a telephone pole
and the house itself;
June Leaf stands just outside this frame,
dressed in a dark overcoat, scarf, beret, gazing out.
The second panel is a rocky snowscape with fir trees
and a slope, partially inside a wooden frame
(which "doubles" the geography).
It has the word YESTERDAY
at the bottom, by definition connoting a "flashback."

The next panel's interior wooden frame holds
nine complete or partial rectangles formed by a wire fence;
through the surface of the complete photograph,
through the wooden frame,
through the wire rectangles,
the eye finally reaches the sea and the sea's horizon.
It feels like a grueling journey to get to the sea,
almost (because of the fence, I think) trespassing—
(perhaps it is better to take in nature at a distance).
The first panel on the second row
exhibits a kind of sculpture—a pickax lain
atop a chopping block—inside the upright wooden frame,
with the sea in the background.
What is written in this panel—FIRE TO THE SOUTH—
might well have chronicled
an actual event, a forest fire, maybe;
at any rate, it takes notice of the world outside Mabou.
The second panel in the second row contains
only about half of a wooden frame;
the landscape inside and outside this frame
holds no people, and snow quilting
the distant headland
is starkly bright compared to the dingier snow
of the foreground.
In the last panel, a man (perhaps a neighbor) stands
frozen like the Tin Man in *The Wizard of Oz,*
except wearing a black jacket,

one mittened hand clutching
the wooden frame itself, as if holding it up—
part of the "surface" inside this frame
has been painted densely dark and shaped
like a tornado or water spout,
as if it is the immediate condition at sea.
Across a black-streaked sky is written,
TO THE EAST AMERICA,
which generally locates the photograph
geographically. Vague, almost hallucinatory
fence posts are lined up along
what possibly is a cliff, the sea in the background.
I love the spaces between these fence posts,
each which appears placed an equal distance from the next.
The sea resides between posts.

After ten years of intense work in filmmaking, Frank returned to still photography in the early 1970s. He fell back on his earlier method of expression for a variety of reasons. In 1972, at the instigation of Kazuhito Motomura and Toshio Hataya [two Japanese publishers], he published a very personal, retrospective examination of his life entitled *The Lines of My Hand....* This book undoubtedly rekindled his interest in his past work and the process of photography in general. In addition, in 1970 Frank and June Leaf, a painter whom he would marry in 1975, bought land in Mabou, Nova Scotia, and that more isolated existence also encouraged a more solitary method of making art. But more than anything else it was the sudden death in 1974 of his twenty-year-old daughter Andrea, coupled with the earlier disappearance and presumed death of his good friend and fellow filmmaker Danny Seymour, that propelled his return to still photography.... Although he did make films that embodied his grief, still photographs became his most immediate and direct means to try "to show how it feels to be alive."

Sarah Greenough
*Robert Frank: Moving Out*

6 p.m., almost dark. I drove to Baddeck,
on the St. Andrews Channel, to use
a bathroom, purchase some cleaning solution
for my binoculars, find a place for dinner.
Minimal necessities and errands of an unhurried day.
In a shop window, I saw an old Smith-Corona manual
typewriter. It was not for sale, it was part of the
window dressing.
Any number of old-fashioned women's and men's hats

were on display, and the ornately lettered sign
announced HATS ARE BACK!
The entire diorama was supposed to evoke the WWII era.
There was a poster warning loose lips sink ships.
(An American poster, I think.)
On the poster, a lithe woman wearing a hat
leaned in to whisper into a man's ear;
he was dressed in a gray suit
and held a swastika-headed cane behind his back.
A schedule of troop transports floated
in the black space at the upper right,
as if it was the woman's thought-balloon.
(How had she obtained such secret information?
She looked to be a proper woman,
whereas he was unmistakably seedy,
had a malevolent grimace.)
At the bottom right, in red block lettering,
it read: THE DEVIL HAS EARS.
Scrolling from the typewriter
was a yellowed sheet of paper
on which someone (perhaps the shop owner)
had begun a letter. There was only the date,
July 8, 1944,
and the salutation, *Dear Mom and Dad.*
In my Robert Frank frame-of-mind, it was
the typewriter that most stood out.
It reminded me of my favorite of his photographs,

"FEAR—NO FEAR, Mabou, Nova Scotia, 1987"
It is idiotic and entirely beside the point
to use the word favorite when referring
to an artist's work so powerful in its range of emotion
and subject.
However, that is my opinion: "FEAR—NO FEAR"
is my favorite. (I can't get it out of my mind.)
Toward "FEAR—NO FEAR"
I delegate a separate (almost *spiritual*) consideration,
or it could be, crudely, acquisition fever.
"FEAR—NO FEAR" is a kind of vertical triptych.
In each panel is a typewriter (the same manual typewriter)
situated on a desk at a window.
The top and bottom frames contain writing,
not the middle.
You can either read it top to bottom (FEAR—NO FEAR)
or bottom to top (NO FEAR—FEAR), depending, I
suppose, on one's existential condition, and because such
is life, that either could be the order
in which a person confronts
(or fails to) any given task or memory, on any given day.
This has always struck me as a photograph about
the daily working life of the artist.
In each frame, the typewriter carriage,
with its rolled-in piece of typing paper,
is at different positions on the horizontal.
A typewriter.

A typewriter in front of a landscape.
The romance of writing, unless one is wealthy,
still has a utilitarian reality.
It is how to make a living.
It requires *tools of the trade,*
including the imagination.
Add nostalgia to the mix, because,
as we know, the manual typewriter
has become a relic.
(A recording of a clacking
manual typewriter, I'm told,
is in the "sound archive" in Washington, D.C.)

Looking at the Mabou pictures, I remembered these
lines of Virginia Woolf: A masterpiece is not the
result of a sudden inspiration but the product of a
lifetime of thought.

Salman Rushdie
*The Ground Beneath Her Feet*

9 p.m., driving back to Mabou. Clear, black sky,
a zillion stars and a full moon.
(Taking the *Bluenose* ferry from Maine

to Nova Scotia one summer, I said to a fellow
passenger, who physically resembled Peter Lorre,
"There's a full moon, you'll be able to read a book
on deck by it." He bet me ten dollars Canadian against.
I handed him my copy of *The Secret Agent* by Joseph
Conrad. An hour out to sea, he sat on a deck chair well away
from electric lights, opened the book, read a moment,
then handed me a ten-dollar bill. When we docked the
next morning in Yarmouth, I looked for him to get my
novel back, but he had "invisibly debarked." [Conrad]
As it happened, I ran into him in front of his hotel in
Halifax a few days later. "I believe you still have my
book," I said, then insisted on following him to his
hotel room, where he handed over the novel. "Gee, not
too generous, are you?" he said. "And right in front of
my wife and kids, too, eh?"
I never felt bad about it. Later, I noticed that he had
written his name on the inside cover, as if he'd made a
ten-dollar purchase.)
As I drove up a hill past a farmhouse, I saw a man
chopping wood by moonlight.
Suddenly I was homesick
for my living room wall, on which hangs
"Mabou (Chopping Wood)" by Robert Frank,
two vertical strips of 8-mm film.
The column on the left
depicts a man holding previous photographs

by Robert Frank
(photographs within the photograph)
upside down and tilted.
The column on the right
depicts a man chopping wood.
It is signed and dated, and also reads,
*Life dances on ...*

Robert Frank has also photographed hospitals, soup
kitchens, people, winter windows, and much more (and
made films) in Nova Scotia; all of these tell his life
and thought there. The landscape photographs contain,
rather than merely evoke, the region around Mabou; the
beaches, sea, sky, which hold on but keep moving.
"What good is intelligence if you cannot discover a
useful melancholy?" the Japanese author Ryunosuke
Akutagawa wrote. Robert Frank's landscape photographs instill in me a melancholy useful because it helps
clarify the world, and equals late autumn.

ABOUT THE AUTHOR

Howard Norman has lived and traveled extensively in Atlantic Canada. His first two novels, *The Northern Lights* and *The Bird Artist,* were shortlisted for the National Book Award. His other novels are *The Museum Guard* and *The Haunting of L.* He received a Lannan Award in fiction and a Guggenheim fellowship. His work has been translated into many languages. A film of *The Bird Artist* is presently in production. Mr. Norman lives in Washington, D.C., and Vermont, and is writing a new novel set in England and Nova Scotia, *What is Left the Daughter.*

The interior text of this book is set in Garamond 3, designed by Morris Fuller Benton and Thomas Maitland Cleland in the 1930s and released digitally by Adobe.

Printed by R. R. Donnelley and Sons on Gladfelter 60-pound Thor Offset smooth white antique paper.

Dust jacket printed by Miken Companies. Color separation by Quad Graphics.

Three-piece case of Ecological Fiber pearl side panels with Sierra black book cloth as the spine fabric. Stamped in Lustrofoil metallic silver.

**NATIONAL GEOGRAPHIC DIRECTIONS**

Featuring works by some of the world's most prominent and highly regarded literary figures, National Geographic Directions captures the spirit of travel and of place for which National Geographic is renowned, bringing fresh perspective and renewed excitement to the art of travel writing.